Meditation

Meditation
a practical study

(With exercises)

Adelaide Gardner

This publication made possible with the assistance of the Kern Foundation

The Theosophical Publishing House
Wheaton, Ill. U.S.A.
Madras, India/London, England

© Copyright 1968 by The Theosophical Publishing House

This is a Quest Book, published by The Theosophical Publishing House, a department of The Theosophical Society in America. The original edition was published by The Theosophical Publishing House, London, England.

First Quest Book edition [revised], 1968.
Fourth Quest Book printing, 1979.

ISBN: 0-8356-0105-6
Library of Congress Catalog Card Number 68-5856.

Printed in the United States of America

ACKNOWLEDGMENTS

This book was written for the Study and Training Committee of the Theosophical Society in England. Very full and grateful acknowledgment is made to the members of the committee for their help throughout. Mrs. Josephine Ransom and Miss Corona Trew, Ph.D., have generously permitted forms of meditation which each had developed to be included in the additional exercises. Miss Grace Raikes gave valuable assistance in revision.

ADELAIDE GARDNER

. . . *If the manas is to perform its proper task of controlling the senses, it must itself reflect the ideal pattern that is laid up in the heavens of the Buddhi. Only when that pattern is reflected in its mirror has it the standard of reference by which to judge. . . nor should we think that the possession of such a divine standard by which to judge attainment is far above us; one to which we may aspire in some dim future. Here and now the Pattern is within us.*

SRI KRISHNA PREM

The Supreme is not really hidden from us, because He cannot hide from Himself, and to think that He can be Hidden from us, who are Himself, is the subtlest of all mayas, is illusion. He is our innermost Self, and the very heart of our being.

ANNIE BESANT

CONTENTS

HISTORICAL SURVEY

Theoretically the practice of meditation is intended to withdraw the personal mind from its persistent preoccupation with worldly affairs, and to train it to concern itself with matters that lead to the understanding of spiritual realities. On examination this simple statement is seen to presuppose the existence of various levels of human thought, and also the ability of man to choose the level to which he will direct attention. Before we can understand the technique of meditation, then, there must be some study of man's nature and capacities. The fact is that, from earliest times, instruction on meditation was preceded and accompanied by the study of the science now called psychology.

Few people realize how very ancient these associated studies are. The following cursory survey of certain aspects of Indian and early European thought is meant to provide the student with a perspective from which the special study that follows can be more clearly viewed. The survey is obviously selective, tracing the history of only one strand of psychological teachings and the use of a certain group of practices.

The similarities of experience that link together the mystics of all periods and religions have been noted and commented upon by great scholars, and students may turn to their works for details of this evidence.* Here we only attempt to outline the continuity of the Indo-European

Varieties of Religious Experience by William James; *Studies in the Psychology of the Mystics* by Joseph Maréchal.

tradition from earliest Indian times down to our own day in regard to the varied levels at which human consciousness expresses itself, and also concerning certain traditional practices by means of which the more spiritual aspects of man's nature may be awakened. Among the latter, meditation in its various forms holds a central position.

Indian philosophic thought is generally considered to have passed through its first formative period at the time of the early Aryan migrations into India. Modern historians give this date variously from 6000 B.C. onward: students of the occult tradition place it far earlier. During the migrations certain ancient hymns came into being, presumably chanted as mantras, or songs of magical effect. Later these were commented upon by the priestly caste, and later still their more profound teachings were expounded by the philosophers of the period. The last phase gave rise to the series of sacred writings known as the *Upanishads*, which are still the kernel of Indian philosophy. All compositions in those days were chanted and transmitted orally from teacher to pupil. In this fashion they passed into the written Sanskrit literature that is India's greatest treasure.*

In the *Upanishads* can be found the essential teachings on meditation that have been used throughout the ages by many of the Indo-European peoples. In the *Taittiriya Upanishad*, admitted to be one of the most ancient, appears the following:

"That which is that bright space within the heart; in that this man resides, innate with mind, transcending death, with brilliancy innate."

There follows an obscure verse that can now be interpreted as suggesting that the pituitary body is "Indra's

Indian Philosophy by S. Radhakrishnan: Vol. I, Introduction—V.

2

birth track," or the point of junction between the inner man and his physical consciousness, and then:

"Self-kingship he attains, lordship of mind he wins, lord over speech, lord over sight, of hearing lord, lord of understanding.

"Then he becometh Brahm, whose body is bright space, whose self is truth, the pleasure-ground of life, in whom mind finds bliss, replete with peace, transcending death. Thus worship then, O thou who for the ancient art hast fit become."*

From this it would seem that the art of self-discipline was already well developed and ancient when the Aryan race reached India.

The Hindu mind enjoys the consideration of abstract material, and the period following the migrations was one in which philosophic speculation appears to have flourished. The Hindu canon of instruction for the search after enlightenment, as it is still called, was well developed by 800 B.C., the approximate date of the Buddha. It was indeed too much classified, too little lived, and had been overgrown by a system of ascetic practices that obscured rather than revealed the purpose of meditation. The princely Seeker sought instruction in the "forest universities" of the ascetics, but went his way onward, finding what he sought not in routine and austerities but in an illumined view of human nature. This led him to see that the root of suffering is human ignorance, especially lack of awareness of the purpose of human incarnation in physical form.

To overcome this deeply ingrained condition of unenlightenment, he devised a formula called the Noble Eightfold Path. The steps on it are in one sense progressive,

*Taittiriya Upanishad: 6; trans. Mead and Chattopadhyaya.

3

though in the end all are needed to reach enlightenment. The first two deal with right knowledge; the next three with right action; and the final three—right effort, right concentration, and right meditation—may be summarized as right mind development. "It seems clear, therefore, that meditation, using the term to summarize the last three stages on the Path, is not merely an integral part of Buddhism, but the very climax of its other doctrines, laws and practices."*

The Buddhist methods of meditation are directed toward overcoming that primal ignorance concerning the purpose of existence which the Buddha held to be the cause of mistaken action, consequent suffering and repeated rebirths. Happiness, the overcoming of all sorrow, is possible. The eightfold path is the way. Meditation as the final teaching of the path was elaborated by the Buddhist brothers and their teachers into a searching and stimulating experience. Its formulation was undoubtedly influenced by various Hindu reformers, but it remains infused and irradiated with the gentle tolerance and beneficence of the Buddhist way of life.†

We pass, rather too quickly, to the Hindu classic view of man and of the practice of meditation, as put forward by the great teachers Patanjali and Shankarâchârya. These Hindu teachings will be given in some detail for various reasons. They are very fully documented in literature that is readily available; they can be provocatively compared both with certain Greek and with modern theosophical ideas; they also throw great light upon some of the modern psychological theories.

*Concentration and Meditation, Buddhist Society, London: Introduction.
†Buddhist Meditation by G. Constant Lounsbery.

One of the most widely studied discourses on the subject of meditation is attributed to the Hindu sage known as Patanjali. Very little else is known about him other than his name. Apparently he codified the ideas of meditation current in the Hindu schools based upon the Sânkhya philosophy. This codification was in verse, could be memorized, and was handed down intact until it took written form. As the *Yoga Sûtras of Patanjali* it has now been translated into many languages.

Leaving aside the question of the date of Patanjali, and of the philosophy behind the teachings, let us pause over his view of man's psychology. This view is stated without religious dogma, for the most part. It is possible to use the methods suggested as a believer, or as an agnostic, provided that the latter has a truly scientific spirit and is determined to discover the nature of his own mind, and of what lies beyond it.*

Patanjali describes the nature of thought and the origin and structure of the personal mind as follows: Man is in essence pure spirit (purusha); the essential man exists both beyond and within the mind. The association of individual human spirits (purushas) with the form of energy called thought (manas), leads to awareness of individual experience—individually perceived sensations, feelings, interior reproductions of the environment—and so to the formation of personal minds. The personal mind is usually just a series of automatic responses and ideas that link a man more or less successfully with his environment. Pure human con-

..*Yoga Sûtras of Patanjali.* The Dvivedi translation published by the Theosophical Publishing House, Madras, India, is accurate. That included in *Yoga and Western Psychology* by G. Coster is probably more intelligible to Western readers. See also *The Science of Yoga* by I. K. Taimni (Quest Book edition).

sciousness (purusha) lies within and beyond the personal assembly of automatisms (vasanas) and is responsible for these, but is not usually able to make the waking brain aware of its existence because the automatisms, heavily charged with feeling (kâma), are so dominant in the field of personal life. Thus while the automatisms remain unchallenged the spiritual man is cut off by them from the waking consciousness. As a result, the personal nature is unhappy, daily life being spent in confused, little-understood incident, and isolated from the discerning interior Self—the ever-existing purusha, the seer. It is ignorance of the true nature and existence of the Self that leads to conduct resulting in pain, pain that—fortunately—in the end leads man to seek for the explanation of his sufferings and so of life itself. If and when the automatisms can be quieted, and the Self discovered behind the conflicting behavior of mind and feelings, fundamental relationships can be understood, and enlightenment and happiness become possible.

In the epigrammatic stanzas of the traditional verse, the sage goes on to tell how the automatisms may be overcome, even when deeply established. He describes the steps the human being has need to take to restore clarity and lucidity to the personal mind, and prepare it for use by the seer as an instrument of cognition. Book III describes the nature of the different kinds of thinking that can be experienced, when control of the physical body, and then of the emotions, permits the clarification of the thinking instrument.

There are in the main four levels or types of knowing, two personal and unreliable, and two of a subtler order. Beyond these lies pure awareness, without ideation. Knowl-

6

edge begins with the critical observation of sensation, and goes on to the observation of psychological experience, stimulated both objectively and subjectively. Both these forms of thinking are of inferior value, and undue attention given to them can hinder clarity of thought. Knowledge of the fundamental laws of nature, together with the capacity to generalize correctly, and to deal with abstract principles, provides a basis from which one can arrive at a clear perception of truth, and when properly developed this leads on to direct awareness of the Self, and of the nature of the universe.

Finally, with perseverance and strict adherence to the impersonal search for reality, the seer can achieve release of consciousness from association with bodily form, and know himself as existing in subtle essence, or even as pure Being. At the conclusion of Book IV it is pointed out that the one who has realized the nature of purusha, which is both the Self and the one interior Essence of which each Self is but a partial expression in time and space, ceases to long for distractions that cloud the mind. "Then the knowable becomes small"—for the Root of all is known.

The work of Shri Shankarâchârya is of even greater repute among Hindu students than that of Patanjali. He is probably the most renowned exponent of the Vedânta philosophy.* Among his many works he left valuable teachings on the nature of the mind, and on methods of reaching illumination. Especially useful for our study is the analysis

*Indian Philosophy as above: Vol. II, Chapter VIII, Sections XIV and XXXV; The Crest Jewel of Wisdom by Shankarâchârya: 88-134, etc.; Atmânâtmâ Viveka by Sankarâchârya, trans., Chatterjee, in Compendium of Râja Yoga Philosophy, edited by Tookaram; The Self and Its Sheaths by Annie Besant; The Pinnacle of Indian Thought by Ernest Wood (Quest Book edition).

of man as a five-fold entity, the elements being readily aligned with those named by Patanjali as the levels of conscious experience.

There is a physical sheath and a vital sheath; the physical body and its vital counterpart which reports sensory stimuli. The third element is the subtle sheath, very complicated but corresponding roughly to instinct, emotion and the ordinary intelligence. Then there is a subtler intelligent consciousness, the sheath of discernment, sometimes called the causal sheath, because it stores the essence of experience. Finally there is the sheath of bliss, the last covering of the Self. This analysis is classic, i.e. it can be found in the *Upanishads* (see quotation on pages 2 and 3); it is also paralleled by the teachings of the Northern School of Buddhism* and reappears almost intact in the teachings of Plato and in modern Theosophy. *(See Chapter II)*

Because Shankarâchârya's works are imbued with the eastern doctrine of the need to free oneself from human limitations and so attain to liberation, it is not easy for the western psychologist to appreciate them at their basic value. But at no time has his analysis of human nature been surpassed, and his influence is noticeable in the succeeding centuries.

The interplay of Indian thought with early European culture has not been recognized until very recent years. The Greek creative period, and the rise of Greek philosophy have been, on the whole, viewed as isolated and strictly European phenomena, but it is now acknowledged that this is far from being the fact. Professor Radhakrishnan quotes Aurobindo Ghose as supporting the idea of a com-

The Secret Doctrine by H. P. Blavatsky, Adyar Edition: Vol. I, 212.

mon source of teaching for the earliest Indian Scriptures and for the line of religious thought that later developed into the Orphic and Eleusinian mystery cults of Greece and Asia Minor.* Professor Radhakrishnan himself is conservative both in his estimate of dates, and in his assumptions and deductions, but Madame Blavatsky supports the idea of an eastern origin for Plato's teachings.†

Those familiar with these subjects will point out that many scholars assign the dates of Patanjali and Shankarâchârya to 600 A.D. or later, and to talk about their influence upon Plato or upon early Christian doctrine is to be guilty of a wide anachronism. However other scholars assign much earlier dates. Students also know that it was usual in India for various successive teachers to take the same name. All that we know about the present sûtras is that someone called Patanjali was probably associated with their final codification at about the given date. It is certain that the material is far older, for it exists in the earliest *Upanishads* and affected Buddhist practices.

Madame Blavatsky in *The Secret Doctrine* frequently states that the inner teachings of Egypt, although derived originally from the far, far West, and hence from the long-forgotten civilization of the Atlantean peoples,‡ were nourished and frequently re-formed through repeated contact with Hindu culture and doctrine. It was by means of the mystery teachings of Egypt that Pythagoras made contact with the wisdom of the East, and it was by this means as well as by the overland contact through Persia that the Greeks received much that was later reinterpreted by the

Indian Philosophy: I, 69-70, edition 1929.
†*The Secret Doctrine:* I, 176; III, 47, 242; IV, 353; V, 36; etc.
‡Plato, *Timaeus:* Introductory conversation; *The Secret Doctrine:* IV, 330; etc.

9

western world.

The clearest proof of the continuity between the eastern traditional teachings and those of Greece comes from the writings of Plato and Plotinus. Although there were certain doctrines which Plato states he had received under the pledge of secrecy, and so could not teach explicitly, he reveals enough to show clearly his contact with the East, and its traditional view of man. The picture of man that is presented in the *Symposium,* the *Phaedrus,* the *Republic,* and finally in the *Timaeus,* leaves no doubt that some sort of link between the Hindu and the Greek doctrines must have existed. For example in the *Republic** the diagrammatic representation of the realms of thought can be readily aligned with Patanjali's analysis. Plato says that the nature of man is such that he uses progressively different kinds of thinking. The process develops from mere conjecture based on sense perceptions through belief in the opinion of others to reasoning and on to the illumined understanding of basic principles. The existence of the one Life in nature, and man's identity with that Life, may well have been an inner teaching of the mysteries, and not to be spoken about too plainly, but it is indicated in the *Timaeus.†* The whole of this very difficult dialogue becomes far more intelligible when read in the light of Shankarâchârya's metaphysics and psychology.

The fourfold sequence leading to ultimate contact with the Real occurs also in the *Symposium,* in the teachings of Diotima regarding the true nature of love, and again in the *Timaeus.* In the *Phaedrus* the fourfold man is likened to a charioteer, with his steeds and chariot—a symbol found in

*Plato, *Republic:* VI, 509D-511E; trans. Cornford.
†*Timaeus:* 90 A, B, C; trans., Cornford in *Plato's Cosmology.*

the early *Upanishads* and frequently repeated in classic Indian literature. The *nous* (Spirit) is the charioteer, whose business it is to control the dual *psyche* (soul), the two horses of which are diverse—one rising upward on powerful wings, the other likewise winged but with a tendency to fall to earth. The chariot is the human body. The gift of wings comes from the divine Eros, the love of truth.* In all this the spirit is entirely Greek, but the idea is an eastern traditional pattern.

In the *Timaeus* a section on the care of the soul gives to each part of man its necessary activities, but "as concerning the most sovereign form of the soul in us we must conceive that heaven has given it to each man as a guiding genius. ...Now if man is engrossed in appetites and ambitions and spends all his pains upon these, all his thoughts must needs be mortal.... But if his heart has been set on the love of learning and true wisdom and he has exercised that part of him above all, he is surely bound to have thoughts immortal and divine...."†

"They must lift up the eye of the soul to gaze on that which sheds light on all things; and when they have seen the Good itself, take it as a pattern for the right ordering of the state and of the individual, themselves included."‡

The influence of Plato and of his Academy lasted until well into the Christian era, and the writings of the great neoplatonist Plotinus acted as a bridge by which much of the same thought passed over into early Christianity, via the early Alexandrian Fathers. G. R. S. Mead has made

*Plato, *Phaedrus*: 245-257.
†*Timaeus*: 90 A, B, C; trans., Cornford in *Plato's Cosmology*.
‡Plato, *Republic*: IV, 441; VII, 540; trans., Cornford.
§*Plotinus* by G. R. S. Mead. Introduction to Bohn Library Edition of *Select Works of Plotinus*.

an interesting comparison between the teachings of Plotinus and those of Shankarâchârya.§ Like all the other great students whom we have quoted, Plotinus held that the practice of virtue and the contemplation of truth lead to the growth of the capacity to enter into direct relationship with the One; this achieved, the alone within oneself may become one with the Alone of the universe.

It is now recognized that, after the closing of the Academy and the dispersal of much of its literature among the universities of the Middle East and succeeding centers of learning in that area, the Greek doctrines revivified Persian philosophy. While these teachings may have found their way to Greece originally from this very area, at this point they returned and were absorbed afresh. Then, via a score or more of Arab, Jewish and Alexandrine philosophers, variants of the Greek, Hebrew and Persian traditions crept back into the Europe of the Middle Ages.

Specialists are busy filling in the details of the reabsorption of classic material by medieval Europe, but the orthodox student is slow to allow for the existence of any hidden tradition involving religious practices and the awakening of the soul to its inner strength. Yet proof that such a tradition exists lies in the genuine alchemical and Rosicrucian writings of medieval and later times. These find their clearest interpretation when viewed in the light of the occult tradition of the East. In the face of the religious ignorance and fanaticism of those dark days, any independent investigations had to be heavily camouflaged or they would have ceased to be possible. This may well account for the obscurity of the philosophic writings of the period.*

The Secret Tradition in Alchemy by A. E. Waite, especially Chapters I and III.

12

Contemporary Christian practice of meditation is touched upon in Chapter III of this book. It follows, in the main, the classic outline, beginning with moral behavior, then mental discipline (prayer) and going on to quietude and the interior identification of the personal life with that of the ideal Being, the Christ.

The genuine seeker, whether in or out of an orthodox group, appears to pass through the same phases of experience, and reaches ultimately the same direct interior illumination and contact with the One. But the literature of modern Christian teachings on this subject is not only much obscured by dogma; it also lacks the psychological background of the earlier writings. Pauline terminology is close to that of Plato, and the *Epistles* have new meaning when this is understood.*

It is interesting that in the development of modern psychology attention is again being drawn to eastern traditional doctrines, although it is natural enough that this should happen. Patanjali and his followers and commentators were fully aware of all that now goes under the name of unconscious thought and feeling, and they had their own methods for dealing with complexes, fixations and the like. There is an increasing literature on the subject of the comparison between eastern and western findings.† Probably the most remarkable parallel is that developed through independent and prolonged observation by Professor Carl Jung. That great psychologist arranged the four phases of analysis in an order that invites close comparison with Patanjali, and the whole age-long tradition of the search for illumination: First comes confession—the re-

The Gospel of Rightness by C. Woods.
†E.g. *Yoga and Western Psychology* by G. Coster.

13

membering and facing of the facts of confused past experience; then the explanation and understanding—the use of the rational mind to appreciate the meaning of the past; then re-education, a period when creative intelligence should be called into play, and the freedom of creative experience not only discovered but used and enjoyed. Finally comes the phase of transformation—for those capable of progressing so far. In this last phase, the "old man" is laid aside, and a new spirit emerges from within, creative, refreshing, bringing to the old life a new vision of its meaning and intention.* Here we find once more the four levels of the Hindu classics, of Plato, and the four stages of the soul's awakening in Plotinus.

It would seem that the psychological teaching derived from the *Upanishads* was not only valid but illumined. Why should this cause surprise? Amidst fossils of limestone dated at least 750,000 years ago the bones of an ape-man have been found, an ape-man *who used fire* (Australopithecus-prometheus). If it took 750,000 years or more to bring man from that condition to his present range of experience, what is a mere 3,000 years or so likely to produce in the way of automatic growth? The significant point is that at the dawn of our Indo-European culture an inspired seer marked out the chart of the way by which a man might deliberately take himself in hand and so travel more quickly toward his far goal. This chart has indeed acted as a guide for many since it was outlined in the early days of India, and there are increasing numbers who will testify that its directions are reliable.

It is true that in modern life there are new problems as

Modern Man in Search of a Soul by C. G. Jung: "Problems of Modern Therapy."

well as new methods of dealing with old material. But the varied nature of the soul of man has not much altered in these few millennia. As Jung so truly recognized, there are still those with primitive intelligence, concerned with the satisfaction of the appetites. There are those of rational mind, often materialistic because the material world is here, immediate, urgent, and with it as background it seems possible to lead a rational existence. There is the seeker after explanations more satisfying than those afforded by the logic of facts, the idealist, with a gleam of inspiration drawn from a glimpse of one or more of the ultimate values—goodness, truth and beauty; he is ready to cherish and feed the winged horse that will lift his chariot into the worlds of inner vision. And—though few—there are still the seekers who know their goal and follow a path that leads them quickly toward it.

For the last two groups it is important to make known that valid religious practices exist, non-dogmatic, perhaps unorthodox for westerners, but of a type used through the centuries by those who seek more light on our recurrent human problems. The practices are progressive, beginning with the endeavor to establish the habit of sound moral and social conduct: such behavior is held to apply to all as a social obligation. For the true seeker, there is further, regular, progressive training, to assist him, first, to understand his own nature and difficulties and the levels at which these are active; and then to develop the quietude of the disciplined mind which, directed toward the real and the true, slowly becomes able to apprehend the underlying meaning and purpose of our scheme of things.

Men differ in their readiness, their aptitude for such practices. A few of special nature can discard forms and use an intensely interior method of self-realization. Others struggle and stumble over the first steps, while the majority need both a sound system and continued practice to establish the hold of the directive Self over the wayward mind. For all types the factor that will determine the effect of the training is the degree of interest, of intense preoccupation, that each brings to the quest.

For this reason unhappiness can be useful. It often forces men on in their search for ultimates.

True happiness can be attained, but its eternal source is within man and not without. By directing attention within, and not wholly without, a doorway opens in what may have hitherto appeared to be a blind wall. Those who learn to pass through that doorway enter a new world.

It is the purpose of this book to explain, in simple modern language, methods of self-training that have been proved by many generations of students to lead to greater insight. The book is a study course with exercises. It presents the facts regarding the mind that need to be known in order to control its use, and it indicates the first essential practices to lay sound foundations for further experiment. Through the use of the methods indicated, and their application in daily life, the soul may be released from its automatic bondage to mundane incident, even while the student learns to live happily, perhaps more successfully than hitherto, with his fellow men. Life in the world is necessary and is intended to stimulate mankind toward the pursuit of wisdom. Yet to live life in such a way that wisdom progressively unfolds itself, it obviously becomes necessary at a certain stage to understand something of the nature of the mind, and of each human being's capacity for self-direction. Meditation is a direct method of arriving at such understanding.

This world of ours desperately needs more people who will concern themselves with ultimate values. Likewise, as many public spirited thinkers are now stating, it deeply needs a richer and more profound understanding of human nature than that found in modern text-books. Such understanding cannot be arrived at by methods of laboratory research, or by taking part in learned academic discussions. It arises primarily from deep perception, from insight, and hence from interior experience. Such insight can be actively stimulated through intelligent use of the discipline called meditation.

Analysis has done much to re-discover the various levels of the human mind, but there is more in man than just a variety of ways of feeling and thinking. The technique of meditation was devised, and still exists, to assist men individually to uncover within themselves that deeply hidden center of the one creative Life that is the divine birthright of every member of the human race. From that center much can be understood that is otherwise obscure. From that level much can be done for the world, for—although our world needs food for its millions of hungry mouths— it needs even more urgently light for the darkness of its myriad human souls.

MEDITATION

A PRACTICAL STUDY
with Exercises

Chapter I

MEDITATION AND ITS PURPOSE

Meditation is the inexpressible longing of the inner man for the Infinite.   *H. P. Blavatsky*
Meditation consists in the endeavour to bring into the waking consciousness, that is, into the mind in its normal state of activity, some realization of the super-consciousness. . . . It is the reaching out of the mind and feelings toward the ideal, and the opening of the doors of the imprisoned lower consciousness to the influence of that ideal.   *J. I. Wedgwood*

The purpose of meditation is the alteration of the polarity of the personal mind, so that it becomes no longer automatically responsive to the emotions and the senses, but rather turns naturally, for stimulus and direction, to the Divine Self, the Root of all.*

The use of meditation for this purpose implies the acceptance of certain principles which are held to be true (see Chapter II). The chief of these is the concept of man as "a god in the making,"† having latent within himself all faculties needed for the understanding of the Divine Life and

*Compare Patanjali's teachings, see p. 5.
†*The Secret Doctrine:* I, 214; V, 449, 452.

its laws; and also having within himself all powers required for his full co-operation with these laws. Another essential principle is that of the twofold nature of the mental world, and of the mind of man.* The mind can either be turned outward to the world of sense to reflect the facts of physical experience, or inward to reflect the realities of spiritual being. Other important principles and facts are also involved, but the purpose of meditation cannot be stated without these two premises. Grant these and the purpose is clear. It is, in the first instance, to wean the personal mind from its habitual attachment to the reports of the physical and the psychic sense organs. Then comes the need to learn to empty it—at will—of its many images, built chiefly from the repetition of sensory experience, "things seen and heard," and distorted by feeling. And then as the mind begins to be controlled, it can be turned as a clear mirror to the world of spiritual reality. "When you have seen these you desire those others no more."†

The goal of meditation is not, however, merely personal self-development. He who pursues this path misses the real objective. The ultimate purpose is to prepare the personal nature so that it is able to reflect and express its relationship with the Universal Self. And once this inner relationship is established, the aspirant can become of real use in the divine plan, for he is then able to bring spiritual wisdom to bear upon daily life.

While this is the goal and purpose of meditation, the methods used, when sound, will bring about noticeable changes in the whole personality. This is a comforting fact, for the complete re-orientation of the mind may easily take

*The Secret Doctrine: II, 47, 48; IV, 210 Footnote; V, 488, 499; The Key to Theosophy by H. P. Blavatsky; Section on "The Septenary Man."
†At the Feet of the Master by Alcyone : Chapter I.

22

several lives to achieve.* Preliminary exercises in concentration can steady and clarify ordinary thought. Determined practice, combined with suitable behavior in daily life, profoundly modifies character. The serenity of mind that arises from success in meditation is an excellent tonic to the nervous system, and also stabilizes the whole psyche in its reactions to daily life. These are results of practical value, and when some proficiency has been gained in controlling thought, it may be used to heal and help others, and to assist public and international work.

While the above statement would be considered to be axiomatic by those who have for many years used meditation as the growing point of their spiritual life, it is only fair to pause a moment to consider certain criticisms frequently heard to the effect that the routine practice of meditation is useless for the awakening of deeper interior awareness.

It is certainly true that so long as one is wholly immersed in one's environment, pleasant or unpleasant, or even if one is just content with things as they are and unwilling to alter either oneself or them, no amount of mental gymnastics will be likely to awaken spiritual insight. Correct observation of external objects can be trained by mere exercises, memory improved, and so on, but routine exercises do not open new centers of awareness.

It is when there is a dissatisfaction with one's way of life, the sense of quest for deeper knowledge, a willingness to adventure into new fields of experience, that such practices are most fruitful. The desire for liberation from the round of birth and death expresses the Buddhist view; the

*For the theory of reincarnation, see *Reincarnation* by Irving Cooper; *Reincarnation* by Annie Besant; and *Reincarnation, Fact or Fallacy* by Geoffrey Hodson (Quest Book edition).

hunger of the soul for God is the Christian term. When a seeker is really hungering for contact with the Divine Nature, he will go on—he will not cease searching until he finds satisfaction for his need. He will attempt deeper realization, test explanations, and try to live in the light of that which he does understand.

But there are many in whom such ardor of intention is not yet awakened, and yet they are desirous of entering upon some sort of quest. They are like workmen who want to use unfamiliar tools; like a student with a good voice but no knowledge of enunciation or of breathing, who wants to be a speaker. For those in such a stage of glimpsing a new interior world, meditation can play a significant part. The technique of mental self-direction can be studied, and in the effort much of value comes to light.

"What a man thinks on that he becomes." This again is from the *Upanishads*. It is obviously true, because thought is always active—stimulating or deadening, creative or repetitive—and ever building its habitual quality into the consciousness of the thinker. Even learning by heart enlarges the repertory of memory, but to be creative new ideas have to be digested and applied, not merely repeated. It is the same with every life process, with all growth. The growth of the soul is no exception. This is the heart of the problem, and a clear understanding of the principles involved in assimilation will clarify the question of success or non-success with meditation exercises.

In eating food, nourishing material has to be selected, eaten regularly, digested. The process of growth that then normally takes place is unconscious. While spiritual progress through the mere repetition of routine may well be said to be an impossibility, the regular use of properly chosen mental exercises provides an aspirant with assimilable mental food. It is the application of the new ideas in daily experience that promotes their assimilation; no amount of meditation upon the Infinite will awaken spirituality in one who forgets the exercise as he leaves his room. The two elements—meditation and its application in life—complement each other, and when used together undoubtedly affect character, can improve health, and may lead to increased capacity to understand and to help others.

The practice of meditation, then, is an effort of the true man to change the habitual, automatic reactions of the personal nature, so that this becomes tranquil and more open to the influence of the spirit. This is contrary to the interests of the personal bodies* for these like the fuss and flurry of strong personal and emotional stimulus—but it is in the direct interest of spiritual awakening. If we cannot see the truth within ourselves, how shall we know the truth about the life around us?

The character of meditation exercises may be varied to suit individual or group work. There are many schools and books recommending special exercises for various purposes. Once the general idea of meditation is understood, all these fall into their natural places.

Those who are seriously interested in this study, and are not already practicing meditation, should arrange for a regular quiet period each day in which to practice some at least of the exercises that will be found at the end of each chapter. If the book is being studied privately each exercise should be used for at least a month. If the subject is being

*Yoga Sutras of Patanjali: Book II. First Principles of Theosophy by C. Jinarajadasa, Chapter VI.

used for group study, and the meetings are fortnightly, or monthly, each exercise can be used during the period covered by the group work on the same section.

Obviously the printed matter may be read without using the exercises at all, or without working over the points suggested for cogitation, but the subject will be far better understood if students and readers make their own experiments and so test the value of the teachings for themselves.

PRIMARY EXERCISE

Arrange to have an uninterrupted period of ten to fifteen minutes. The best time is in the morning, preferably after bathing and doing some easy breathing exercises, but any time between 4 a.m. and 10 p.m. will do. Late evening meditations are not advisable.

Each night choose a subject for meditation the next morning. A list of suitable books is given below.

At the chosen hour sit upright in a comfortably restful position. Relax the eyes, the back of the neck, the shoulders and the back, while keeping the spine erect.

Relax the muscles of the thighs, the knees and the feet. Let the weight of the body sink into the seat. It may take at least five minutes to become relaxed, but it is important to practice relaxation until it is habitual.

When the body is relaxed, turn the mind quietly to the subject chosen. This may be a virtue, or a sentence. Try to hold the mind to that one idea for at least three minutes, remaining relaxed. Remember that concentration is not a matter of physical effort.

Take a few deep breaths, stretch the body fully, and return slowly to normal activity.

This exercise should be repeated regularly, even if it seems dull. Good physical relaxation is a fundamental in learning to control the body, the emotions and the mind.

POINTS FOR CONSIDERATION

(1) The two principles named, at the beginning of the chapter, as basic to the practice of meditation, need careful consideration. The concept of man as a god in the making will be found fully discussed in *Gods in Exile* by J. J. van der Leeuw. The two-fold nature of

the mental world is expounded in *The Key to Theosophy,* reference on page 22.

(2) Consider why meditation brings about noticeable changes in the personality.

(3) Why is relaxation so important? What is it that induces tension in the body? Can one relax tensions in the emotional and mental nature as one relaxes them in the physical body? What element of the higher Self is needed to do this? (See page 35, Chapter II.)

(4) Consider both the value of regular meditation and its failure in some cases to alter either experience or character. Look for the principles involved in the successful practice, and those governing the failures.

GENERAL READING LIST FOR THE SUBJECT AS A WHOLE

Meditation for Beginners	J. I. Wedgwood
Concentration, An Approach to Meditation	Ernest Wood
Concentration and Meditation	Published by the Buddhist Society, London
Thought Power	Annie Besant
Gods in Exile	J. J. van der Leeuw

Special reading will be suggested for each chapter.

SUITABLE BOOKS FOR DAILY STUDY AND MEDITATION

At the Feet of the Master	Alcyone
The Bhagavad Gîtâ	Hindu Classic
Flowers and Gardens, In His Name. Is and Is-to-be, What We shall Teach, etc.	C. Jinarajadasa
The Kingdom of Happiness	J. Krishnamurti
A Year of Grace, Anthology	Published by Gollancz

Chapter II

ESSENTIAL BACKGROUND

*There is a self that is of the essence of matter—
there is another inner self of life that fills the other
—there is another inner self of mind—there is another inner self of truth—knowledge—there is another inner self of bliss.*

Taittiriya Upanishad

Meditation is practiced for very different reasons, chiefly
determined by temperament. One person likes quiet, while
another values the opportunity to dwell on a special ideal,
personal or impersonal. Some are filled with devotion and
aspiration toward a special teacher, and lift themselves into
his presence by sheer identification with him.

Here meditation is being considered as a spiritual
science, the age-old science of training the personal nature
so that it can express the life of the spirit. The system has
many variants, and can be approached from many angles.
While devotion is a powerful aid in its practice, it is not
essential. Devotion lends wings, but it is possible to walk.
For fruitful use of the method with or without devotion,
it is important to have a fairly clear understanding of the
elements involved and especially of the nature of the
personality that is being trained, and of the powers of the
spirit that it is hoped may be awakened and expressed.

In what follows it will be assumed that the reader already has some acquaintance with elementary theosophical teachings, and is familiar with the idea of the sevenfold universe, man's various bodies, and the general occult scheme of evolution.* Only certain elements of those teachings that are especially involved in the study of meditation will be examined in the course of this study.

The human spirit is an expression of the one Life that supports and maintains our universe; when perfected it is in fact the most complete expression of that Life within our system, for it can become fully conscious and creative. Man is not a creature, a created being; he is a spirit, a direct emanation of the Divine Word. His bodies are created, formed under the laws of action and reaction with the help of nature's invisible helpers. But the human spirit has within it a spark of that which Is: it exhibits in itself, in small, the pattern of the Divine Creator.

The true human being, called in theosophical terminology the ego, is triple in nature, having the powers of choice (will, *âtmâ*), insight (intuition, *buddhi*), and abstract thought (higher *manas*). This ego comes into existence at a given moment, when a spark of the one Life is able to link itself to a highly-developed animal mind, and to polarize the whole animal consciousness toward itself for its own use.† Shankarâchârya called this element in man *the causal body*, for it becomes the causal center of all the sequent human incarnations, and the storehouse of all human experience.

*For general treatment of these points see such books as *First Principles of Theosophy* by C. Jinarajadasa; *Elementary Theosophy* by Rogers; etc.

†*First Principles of Theosophy*: Chapters III, VI, VII; *Study in Consciousness* by Annie Besant: Chapter XI; For Shankarâchârya's teaching, see "Historical Survey."

The animal mentality, feelings and instincts, together with a now upright physical form, give man what are called his personal bodies in theosophical terms. These have all been developed in the lower kingdoms of nature, and are filled with earthiness, with so-called lunar forces, the atavistic tendencies of the psychologist. The triple spirit, the ego in man, is solar, shining outward, self-sustained, creative. Thus there is an inevitable conflict in man because of his dual structure, and much has been written about this in religious literature. In orthodox terms the spirit is said to be able to regenerate the bodies, meaning that the personal nature may be disciplined and hence made subservient to the spiritual. This is a long process.

It begins when the fully developed animal consciousness becomes linked to a causal human center at individualization. The ego can then reach down and express itself through the embryonic mind, the feelings, instincts and physical habits of the animal bodies. The combination forms rudimentary man, now ready and eager for further mental awakening and development. In the occult view it is for this purpose that the animal has been developed in the long ages of its past—just to provide a human ego with the means of living consciously in the three densest levels of our system, those of thought, feeling and action.

The ultimate purpose of this marriage between the triple spiritual Self and the denser bodies is that the Self, through acting as permanent center for many human incarnations, shall gradually be awakened and extended until it can express its full creative awareness on all levels of human experience. The divine Spark needs the provocative stimulus provided by conscious contact with the denser worlds to enable it to evoke, and learn to use, all that is latent within it. Man is indeed a "god in the making": the grandeur of his future is without limit.* The occult teaching is "become that thou art!"

To reach his far goal, however, man has to develop, train and refine the personal bodies acquired at individualization, and this is not to be done in one life or even in a score. The early development of the bodies tends to make them strong and self-centered but not centered in the true Self. By the time that serious meditation is attempted, the personal nature—ordinary thought, personal feeling, and so on —is usually well expanded and expresses normal human thinking, feeling and action easily if not skillfully. But the focus of chief interest has become fixed in the "false I," the temporary, somewhat isolated representative of the Self that is the center of each incarnation.

Moreover, each body has a consciousness of its own, usually called the physical, emotional and mental elementals. These, formed of elemental essence, are all on the downward arc of involution, seeking denser forms for their expression.† Hence they enjoy gross living, excitement, and similar activities which do not help toward spiritual experience.

To train the bodies as tools of the spirit, the student has now to choose the new habits he wills to develop, and to train the elementals to accept them. The new way of life will permit association with finer grades of elemental life, while the coarser are thrown out to learn lessons elsewhere.

One reason why meditation becomes mere routine, and hence ineffectual for many who practice it, is that they are unwilling to alter old habits of eating, sleeping, breathing,

*See reference page 21, Chapter I.
†See reference page 25, Chapter I.

behavior in general, and are especially unwilling to change established ways of thinking and feeling. So, for example, however much an aspirant may cultivate goodwill and tenderness of heart, expressing it perhaps toward animals or children, nevertheless if hostility toward those whose opinions differ from his own is allowed to remain unchallenged, the character of such an aspirant will not be materially altered.*

When a choice has to be made, large or small, it is a very useful thing to get the habit of viewing it from the point of view of the significance of the choice for the spiritual nature. Is this action, feeling, thought, merely the result of an old habit, and desired as such by strongly ingrained nature—that is by the elemental life of the bodies, or is it aligned to what I begin to see as the spiritual view of life?

It is helpful, in dealing with the bodies as a whole, to get clear in one's mind the illusory nature of *all* sensation, not only the reports of the physical senses, but also of the psychic. All the senses play tricks of illusion; only a critical examination of their reports on the part of the higher intelligence will differentiate fake information from underlying facts. For example, certain shades of blue will look greenish if placed near yellow; the same tone will appear bluish if placed near pink. This is evidence that sensations depend upon environmental factors. They likewise are affected by the interest and the fatigue of the observer.

The effect of environment, fatigue, conditioning of all kinds, is even more marked on the psychic sense, because of the shifting quality of the material in which this works, and the intimate effect of feeling and thought upon the very mechanisms used to observe psychic matters. The

*See Chapter VI on "Obstacles" for further material on this point.

psychic world is continually called the "world of illusion" in occultism, both for this reason and also because it is so personal and so easily distorted by egotism and self-concern. The impersonality demanded for successful meditation, as a spiritual exercise, is fortunately also the best possible training for the right understanding of psychic phenomena, and for testing flashes of psychic experience that may occur from time to time.

Alert criticism of the senses, and of all material presented by experience for consideration, is called *discrimination* as to the real and the unreal. This is one of the sensitive qualities that the mind needs to develop, in order to be an accurate servant of the spirit.

The dual nature of the mental world was noted in the previous chapter. It is the nature of the mind stuff, the material of the mental world, to take the shape of any impulse that is presented to it. The fact that the mind (manas) reflects *two* levels of experience within itself *with equal ease* needs to be pondered and assimilated. The two uses of the mind in man, the one dealing with objective happenings, the other with abstract ideas, provide an important clue that can lead to evoking the conscious activities of the spirit.

It is common experience that the objective mind associates itself readily with the reports of the senses, with feelings, and with memories and plans involved in daily living.* It is not so fully recognized that the subtler level of mind turns just as easily and naturally to the buddhic life, and is immediately responsive to wide vision, to impersonal ideals, and to genuine intuitions. The quality of thought associated with the subtle mind, its sense of

Patanjali: Book I, 1-11, Dvivedi commentary.

34

wholeness and its intuitive understanding, can be brought through to ordinary waking consciousness if attention is turned regularly every day for a given time to the subjects with which it naturally deals. Some time, if only twenty minutes even on a journey, should be arranged when the personal mind can be left aside, quiescent, while the waking self reads about, and considers, subjects that are impersonal, philosophic, and of general—not personal—interest.

As stated earlier, the spirit in man has other great powers which may also be awakened and expressed in daily life. The sense of unity (buddhi) grows when we really love others more than ourselves, try to serve others intelligently, and seek to understand those who are most unlike ourselves. The creative power of the will (âtmâ) is awakened through the tackling of difficult matters, and strengthened by persistence in carrying any task undertaken through to a reasonable conclusion. *The will is also exercised by deliberately letting go.* Physical relaxation is a true exercise of the will, a release of strain through poise and inner stillness.* The voluntary renunciation of our claims upon others, of clamorous feelings and the like, constitutes the relaxation of the emotional nature. The mind is relaxed by learning to rest quietly in one thought, or one condition. Such exercises cleanse and train the bodies, and awaken the spiritual will.

Quiet in the personal nature helps the growth of the higher mind, for the peace of the spirit can be known only when the emotional self is still. The attainment of personal

*There are various books on relaxation, but not always easy to secure. *You Must Relax* by Jacobson is reliable and thorough; *Power Through Repose* by A. P. Call gives simple exercises. See also Chapter VI, p. 71.

quietude promotes *detachment* in the personal bodies, and detachment is another quality much needed for success in meditation.*

These two significant factors, discrimination and detachment, are given varying names by different teachers. From the Patanjali sûtras they are usually translated as direct effort and non-attachment. Another version gives determination and self-recollection. The Buddhist term for discrimination is the equivalent of "opening the doors of the mind," that for dispassion is "preparedness for action," or learning to live rightly for its own sake and for no other reason. In essence the one implies an awakening of the spiritual will; the other a progressive withdrawal from entanglement in personal feelings.

The general attitude required as background for the successful use of meditation may be summed up as follows. First comes a growing appreciation of man as essentially spiritual in nature, with immense creative powers which are latent, waiting for suitable means of expression. There follows an understanding of the illusory, separative, and generally self-interested habits natural to the personality, which has grown up from below, and knows no better. A willingness to subdue these personal habits, and to alter them for the sake of larger spiritual experience, needs to be backed by persistence, since one is now setting out to accomplish something quickly for which others may take many lives of slow growth, drifting a little forward, then backward and forward again. Combined with the training of the personality, and the attempt to make it simpler and

*Discrimination and detachment are helpfully discussed in *At the Feet of the Master*. For the care and training of the bodies see *Introduction to Yoga*, by Annie Besant.

more beautiful, should come the lifting of the attention to the things of the spirit, and it is this that will arouse most quickly the positive activities of the ego, its will, its insight, and its ever-present love for, and willingness to serve, humanity as a whole. When his interest and attention are aroused, the spiritual man becomes more active and lends powerful help in changing the bodies to meet his now recognized needs. It is part of the work of meditation to make a daily link between the aroused spirit and the still resistant personality. At such times the personality is stilled and listens, and the inner consciousness can make itself felt as peace, strength and wisdom.

EXERCISE SUGGESTED—FOR GROUP OR PERSONAL USE

Seated quietly as suggested previously, let the body be relaxed.

Say: (or think definitely, in each case) My body is relaxed, resting. *Breathe quietly and steadily and let the body become more and more quiet. Say:* My body is relaxed, but I am not the body. *Pause.*

Say: My emotions are becoming quiet. *Feel kindliness, good will, as far as possible, to all. Let the sense of peace and quietude soak into the soul. Say:* My emotions are stilled, but I am not the emotions. *Pause.*

Say: My mind is to become quiet. *Think of some wide view, as from a hill top, or over an expanse of the sea. Let the mind expand slowly, without excitement, opening itself to silence and to peace. Say:* The mind is still, receptive, but I am not the mind. *Pause.*

Say: I am the Self; strong, pure, filled with light and life, one with all other selves. *Rest in this idea. If preferred, turn in homage to the ideal of the Christ, or of a special Master. Try not to think in words, but to enter into peace.*

Return in consciousness to the mind, cleansing it with the life of the Self.

Return to the emotions, feeling them sweet and strong.

Return to the physical body, taking several quiet deep breaths, feeling it refreshed and strengthened.

Get up quietly from this exercise, and hold its interior peace in the heart, even when active in daily work.

POINTS FOR CONSIDERATION

(1) Consider the type of study and reading that helps to prepare the mind for meditation; should it be intellectual, devotional, or both?

(2) What is a personal elemental? What is its nature and

why is it said to be on the involutionary path? (See reference, page 25.)

(3) What is the nature of the conflict between the life of the spirit, and the life of the personality? When is this conflict likely to be the most intense—in early or in later periods of human evolution? Give examples of this conflict in daily life.

(4) Give some time to considering the terms control, training, refining, in regard to the bodies. How are these practices helped by relaxation of tension?

(5) In what ways can a recognition of the life of the spirit help us in daily life?

BOOKS FOR STUDY

At the Feet of the Master	Alcyone
Introduction to the Study of Yoga, Lecture I	Annie Besant

Chapter III

VARIOUS METHODS

*The ways to God are as many as the breaths in the
bodies of men.*   *Sufi Saying*

Meditation is an accepted practice in nearly all religions,
but during long periods of time and under different cul-
tures it is natural that varying methods should have been
developed. The variations may be classified according to
temperament, technique, or the religious outlook that
gives color to the system.

An analysis of the use made of meditation according to
the different religions is not easy, because members of
each religion belong to every type, and use methods sympathetic to their personal bias. The following paragraphs
indicate the differences in emphasis, but every religion includes a variety of practices.

The *Hindu* faith acknowledges as valid six different sys-
tems of philosophy, and includes many sects devoted to
special gurus or teachers, or to aspects of the one truth. All
forms of yoga are used in this vast and inclusive group.
For many the object of devotion is Sri Krishna, worshipped
as the Lord of Love. Meditation upon his birth as a help-
less child, and upon the phases of his life on earth, lead to
mystic union with him.

Buddhist practice is directed toward freeing the personal

41

nature from the ignorant habits of mind and body that bind man to rebirth. This involves the study and understanding of the Good Law, the observance of which leads to liberation from recurrent incarnation.

There is a systematic and complete series of meditations upon aspects of the Law, upon qualities to be cultivated and avoided, upon peace, death, the divine states, and so on. The following of the middle way is the keynote of the practice. Northern and Southern Buddhism are very different in their teachings.

Islam is essentially a religion of devotion, and—like the Christian faith—is centered upon devotion to one Teacher. It is a way of life that can be full of inspiration for the man of action and for the mystic. A well-known mystical group within this religion is that of the Sufis, but mysticism is not altogether characteristic of this faith.

The teaching of the majority of *Christian* religious bodies is more concerned with the offering of verbal prayers and praise, formal or extempore, than with silent meditation, although there are certain groups, notably the Society of Friends, which have no rituals and both recommend and use an entering into the silence. There is, however, a great deal of Christian literature, both classic and modern, on the subject of meditation, and in many religious communities the science of meditation is fully understood and practiced.

One of the Christian methods is to begin with meditation upon the events in the life of Jesus of Nazareth. It is based upon the cycle of the Christian year, and its aim is to cultivate certain emotions and virtues evoked by the contemplation of the Christ life. In the more advanced stages there is an entering into the consciousness of the Christ in mystic union, allowing oneself, through devotion, to be transformed into his likeness. Prayers and the use of the rosary may be employed to assist interior stillness, while meditation upon, or during, the Eucharist assists in the realization of the interior Christ.

On temperamental lines a general distinction can be made between the approach to meditation natural to those called mystics, and to others termed occultists. The difference between the two is easily exaggerated, but it does exist in all religions, especially in the earlier stages of spiritual discipline.

The mystic is inclined to be simple and direct in his intellectual approach to religious matters; strong devotion and single-mindedness are his keynotes. His method is, through devotion, to lift his consciousness into unity with the one Life as shown in his ideal. He identifies himself with the life of that ideal, which may be either personal or impersonal.

The occultist is inclined to be scientific in his outlook, and has the same approach to spiritual matters. He studies the laws of nature, including the laws affecting human consciousness, and brings an inquiring mind to bear on religious study and practice.

It is sometimes said that the occultist is more tolerant than the mystic, while the latter exhibits greater enthusiasm and self sacrifice; each type has the faults that go with its strong qualities. It is probable that, toward the end of training, the two paths merge. The system of meditation used will vary at different stages for each type, but the occultist will tend to use methods requiring study and self-analysis, while the mystic prefers dedicated action, introspection and the more contemplative forms of meditation.

An analogy may help to clarify the difference and likeness of these two natures. The occultist, in attempting to climb the inner stairway of his consciousness, travels step by step, understanding the stages of the process through which he is passing. The mystic experience is an immediate one, as though carried upward in an elevator. But each, in the end, must learn something of the other's method of travel or his experience will not be complete.

The most complete known analysis of spiritual training is found in the seven schools of yoga exercises recognized in Hindu practice. They are given here to show the varieties of meditation that are helpful to different types.

(a) *Hatha yoga* works upon the physical body, using physical discipline as a means of awakening the spiritual will. The breath is controlled and difficult postures are practiced, in order to break the body, to train it as a horse is trained to obey its rider, the rider in this case being the spiritual man. Mental exercises are combined with these physical postures. Such practices can affect the vital body and the psychic centers, and sometimes lead to enhanced consciousness, but they are easily misused and then become subject to special dangers.*

(b) *Mantra yoga* is the chanting of sacred phrases with devotion and concentrated attention. It aims at tuning the personal nature to a subtler keynote than the ordinary waking consciousness, so that it may "hear" the Voice of the Silence, the Word, God's utterance of his own identity. The right use of varied mantras is a profound science, but many a devotee uses only one.

(c) *Laya yoga*, the yoga of fire, aims at arousing the mys-

The Chakras by C. W. Leadbeater: Section on "Danger of Premature Awakening of Kundalini."

terious creative power of kundalini, and special mental and physical exercises are prescribed for this purpose. If kundalini can be rightly directed to the psychic and spiritual centers in the body, a release of the divine creative power takes place. "Nature is wholly regenerated by fire."

(d) Karma yoga is the yoga of action or work; duty done for its own sake without desire for fruits, such as the reward of success or approbation, and without disappointment in case of failure. The aim is skill in action, and the training of all the bodies to respond to the will of the Self. It may be said to be a considerably modified, and certainly a safer, form of hatha yoga. The meditation recommended is absorption in the task in hand, and single-minded concentration upon it. Formal meditation at fixed times may be used, partly to recall the consciousness to its ideal purpose, and also to train the bodies in efficiency and impersonality.

(e) Bhakti yoga concentrates its efforts on devotion to an ideal and upon the love of God, or of a special spiritual teacher. Symbols, ritual, organized worship, mantra, may all be used as aids to the attainment of union with the divine. This is the way of many religions and usually of pure mysticism, without the use of rituals. Forms of meditation vary, but always include a period in which the consciousness is identified with the ideal.

(f) Jnâna yoga, the yoga of discrimination, consists in developing a progressive discrimination between the real and the unreal, between the One, and the many forms It assumes. It aims at knowledge of the Self, attained by clear thinking and hence by a clarified perception of the whole scheme of manifestation. Methods of meditation vary as the inner vision opens, but they include the effort to dis-

cern the truth about the various activities of the personality, in order to reach conscious union with the Self. Regular study is considered essential to train and to expand the mental consciousness.

(g) Râja yoga, meaning royal or kingly yoga, is the most inclusive of all these eastern forms. It requires no belief or acceptance of dogma, and may be undertaken in a spirit of pure experiment. Its aim is the complete stilling of the personal life, leading to Self-realization. This necessitates the relaxation of physical tensions, and the development of emotional non-attachment and mental quietude, in order to achieve a completely harmonized personality under the control of the spiritual will. It is a system much favored by those undertaking serious occult training. The forms of meditation employed again vary with the need of the individual and his stage of growth, but they are closely allied to those used for jnâna yoga.

In so brief a survey there are necessarily many omissions, but the above will serve to illustrate the extremely wide variety of methods employed in the practice of meditation throughout the ages.

EXERCISE SUGGESTED

Experiment with the exercises suggested previously will have given the student an idea of some of the difficulties that lie in wait for him who would establish effective control over his mind. This section will have shown him the wide diversity that exists in regard to method. It is at this point that he should practice, for some time, a basic exercise that is an acknowledged foundation stone for all forms of mental training. It is called the practice of recall. The exercise provokes the natural resistance of the mind to enforced discipline, while teaching the student the best method of overcoming that resistance.

In his book *Concentration, An Approach to Meditation*,* Mr. Ernest Wood devotes a chapter to this exercise, and this should be read if possible. The following is a summary of the practice.

Instead of attempting to hold the mind fixedly upon one subject, or quality, choose a central idea and then let the mind dwell on all sorts of thoughts associated with the idea chosen. But the moment touch is lost with the central point, call the attention back, and start afresh with the same topic. In doing so *follow the train of thought backward* to the point at which it left the chosen topic.

For example: the object selected is the face of a watch. With physical eyes closed, the mind pictures the watch clearly and is then allowed to think of time, of hours and minutes (as measured by the watch), of the length of the hands, of other types of watches (in comparison with this watch), and perhaps at that point the mind jumps to elegant watches of earlier centuries, to clothes of various periods, to the French Revolution...and the student real-

*Quest Book edition.

47

izes that he has lost contact with the original object. He is thinking of past lives, of all sorts of things, but not of the watch-face.

So he must *work backward:* past lives, French Revolution, period clothing, elegant watches—step by step—until he has returned to the timepiece in his hand. It may sound a simple thing to do, but when five minutes can be spent without losing contact with the central theme, one has learned something about thought control.

Mr. Wood also suggests that the practice is helped by a positive attitude toward daily life. Choose what you will do; do it without complaint; alter your choice if you think best, but *sustain effort willingly.* If life appears to be made up of activities that are all equally uncongenial, one has at least a choice as to the order of their doing. Concentrate on what you are doing, and avoid day-dreams, wishful thinking, and idleness that is not creative. Such a life clarifies the mental and emotional life. It simplifies one's automatic reactions and brings these into harmony with the will of the Self.

POINTS FOR CONSIDERATION

(1) Does it help to consider oneself a mystic or an occultist? Is there any value in knowing one's natural type of approach?

(2) What is the value of devotion to a personal teacher or leader, when unable to be in the physical presence of that teacher? How does the spiritual quality of the teacher affect the relationship?

(3) Why is meditation upon centers in the nervous system, or upon psychic chakras, held to be dangerous? (See reference, page 44.)

(4) If meditation is a science, should not everyone approach it in the scientific spirit? Is meditation also an art?
(5) What is meant by meditation "through absorption in the task in hand?"
(6) Consider the following quotation: "It is an aspect of our amphibious situation that one part of our being can never be purified apart from the other." *The Golden Sequence* by Evelyn Underhill.

BOOKS FOR STUDY

Practical Mysticism	Evelyn Underhill
Buddhist Meditation	G. Lounsbery
Self-Realization through Yoga and Mysticism	J. Ransom

Chapter IV

PROGRESSIVE STAGES: CONCENTRATION

Success in the spiritual life is gained less by fierce wrestling with the lower nature than by growing into the knowledge and appreciation of higher things.

MEDITATION FOR BEGINNERS *J. I. Wedgwood*

In the curious, inverted way that is characteristic of so much personal experience, the idea of thought control is often misconceived as a process by which a student strains and labors to direct thought into channels that are unaccustomed and difficult. Such an approach tends to make the effort very complicated, and confuses the issue. The thought world, in fact, provides a very free, responsive medium, when left to itself. The personal mind, built of the material of the thought world, responds equally readily to the reports of the senses or to the intuitions of the spiritual Self.

It is only because of long-established habit that the ordinary human mind pays more attention to the reports of the senses, and to memories of "things done and to be done" than it does to the larger issues of the spiritual life. And the personal habits that encourage the usual type of thought—such as the constant identification of oneself with the physical body and its needs and ways, or reacting with strong feeling to other people's behavior—arise in the desire nature more than in the mind. The mind, however, willingly maintains all such habits by supplying chain-series of mental pictures which keep the desire nature stimulated and dominant.

To develop control of thought, it is the established habits of this personal psyche—that is of the mental-emotional team which has for so long worked together—that need to be observed and challenged. The pattern of their behavior has to be broken up and re-formed on an altogether different design. During this process, which is usually a long one, and achieved in progressive stages, the mind gradually returns to its pure state. The clearer and simpler the mind body becomes, the more the heights of the spiritual consciousness can be reflected within it. Where formerly there was only a succession of imperfect images provoked by personal desire, now something of truth, even of reality, can be interiorly discerned.*

Effort there must be: one learns little unless one is willing to persist in boring, and for the moment apparently useless, attempts to change the focus of attention. Most people are not accustomed to using the will in order to remain concentrated in thought on a given subject. But the effort is similar to that of learning to ride or to skate or to do anything else with one's personal nature. One is using a new set of muscles, as it were, and they only become skilled in the desired action after some time spent in sustained effort toward learning the new technique. As the technique is mastered the action becomes, first, effortless and then more or less automatic.

In dealing with the three generally accepted stages in

*See "The Lake of Beauty" and "Desirelessness" by Edward Carpenter, *Towards Democracy*.

the practice of thought control, the student should first make clear to himself that the terms used to describe these stages are of less concern than the progressive experience that is implied in the sequence. Various writers use the terms in different order, or give the stages different names, but on close study one finds that the sequential experience described is usually the same. It so happens that for a student who is beginning to observe the behavior of his own thought processes, the attempt to concentrate attention upon a definite object is useful, not in itself, but as a means of discovering the way that thought and will can work together, and also of observing the nature of his own habitual feelings. So also it is a fact, discovered by many repeated and independent experiments, that further exercises follow effectively in a certain sequence. Those pinning the attention to one point come at the beginning, and those that expand the mind, letting it open itself quietly to the uttermost bounds that consciousness can reach, are more fruitful after a certain preparation for such quietude has been made.

In this study we shall use the terms concentration, meditation and contemplation in that order. Technically, concentration is the holding of the mind to a single idea at will. It involves freeing the mind from habitual association with desire and feelings, through exercises that reveal its prejudiced and wandering ways, and then focusing it quietly on a single thought. The will is brought to bear upon the mind, especially through the choice of impersonal objects for such concentration, objects without emotional associations.

In meditation thought is led to rest quietly on a concept that has many overtones. The overtones and associations are allowed to fill the whole consciousness, so that nothing is experienced save the one concept, with all its richness. Such meditation is known as meditation "with seed"; that is, it is concerned with a given idea and results in further mental activity, leading to deeper understanding. It can be sub-divided into various steps, or degrees of development.

Contemplation is meditation "without seed," an entrance into a wordless state in which all that is ordinarily known as thought ceases. This condition is practically beyond verbal consideration.

CONCENTRATION

Much that is admirable has been written on this subject, and Mr. Ernest Wood's *Concentration, An Approach to Meditation* is to be especially recommended, since it gives useful hints and a detailed series of exercises covering six to nine months.

It is worth while to put strong emphasis upon the importance of relaxation of body, and of quiet easy breathing, in relation to exercises in concentration, because when trying something new it is usual to become tense with the effort. What is needed, however, is a withdrawal from tensions and fretting of all kinds. The act of deep breathing if easy and without strain, associated with relaxation of nerves and muscles, definitely assists the quieting of the mind.*

The following is a good sequence for the beginning of any period of concentration. The object upon which one is to concentrate having been determined previously, begin by relaxing the body, being sure that it is at ease and comfortably placed. Take a few easy deep breaths, while allow-

*See reference on p. 35.

54

ing body, feelings and mind to become peaceful. Then assert clearly that for the next few moments one is concerned only with the single matter in hand, that of learning to bring thought under the control of the inner Self. This provokes a condition of "recollectedness," in which the whole consciousness is drawn together and prepared. The preparation made, the mind is then turned to the object chosen and kept upon it for the agreed period.

The objects first used for concentration should be entirely impersonal and objective, not a flower or a color or anything that has emotional associations. This is an exercise to reveal the ways of the mind and, during early experiments, thought needs to be—so far as possible—isolated. The unfamiliarity of so isolating thought from feeling often causes boredom or irritation. Students will say: "It would be so much easier to concentrate on something that has interest, rather than on a pencil or an eraser or a match." And that is the moment to realize that the exercise is devised for training in the use of the will, through the sustaining of a deliberate choice, quite as much as it is for studying the behavior of thought.

No attempt, however, should be made to use the human will in a too positive manner to *force* attention. Its natural use is that of a deleting agent, by which all that interferes with a given project is quietly erased or brushed aside, leaving the field clear for the chosen activity. The will in man should be sharply distinguished from desire, which is its reflection and counterpart at the personal levels, and a most useful element in human growth. But desire is always for that which is external to the consciousness, at one level or another, while the will works from within outward— not drawn out, but of its own power. It is a very quiet, deeply interior human attribute.*

This quietude of the will is partly due to its being an inhibitive force rather than one that acts positively. Desire grasps, drives, pushes into action. The will, when rightly used, merely brushes aside all obstacles, clears the field, and leaves a space free where the mind can observe or create. This is an important principle, one that is not easy to understand intellectually. It is well illustrated by the relation of the will to relaxation. In relaxation there is merely an inhibition of all tension; one neither flexes the muscles nor extends them, one just *lets go*. This is perhaps the best and most direct illustration of the will as an inhibitive or deleting agent. It *permits* relaxations; it *permits* quietude of mind.

So when the psyche becomes restive at being enforced for three minutes to consider a single, unemotional object, the student should use the will quietly to hold the field of attention free from feeling, free from intruding ideas. "Not that, not that." The mind is then left to rest upon the chosen idea, and when it begins to feel assured, the interruptions will cease. If and when the mind succeeds in breaking loose and wandering, the student may use the technique described in the exercise for Chapter III to follow its track back to the chosen subject.

A valuable concentration exercise is to count the breaths, breathing easily, but as slowly *as can be maintained without physical strain*. The mind is merely to be kept on the nor-

Personality and the Will by Aveling; Chapter V. Describes various experiments to investigate the nature of the will in action. It was shown that effort, striving, ceases as and when the true will acts. Pure willing is cold, calm, certain, and can act contrary to instinct or established habit. See also *Study in Consciousness* by Annie Besant, Part II, especially Chapter VII.

mal act of breathing and the breaths counted up to ten, and then up to ten again. When thirty breaths can be counted without any other thought except that of breathing, something about concentration of attention has been mastered. On no account should the breath be held, or made abnormal, and persons suffering from heart difficulties should not use this exercise. If slight tension appears to result, relax the body still more fully, or drop the exercise. This is an old Buddhist practice, used for centuries by Buddhist monks, some of whom can maintain concentration for three hundred slow breaths—about three hours!

Regular use of any simple concentration exercise almost immediately reveals the automatic entanglement of thought and feeling in personal affairs, as well as the skilled responsiveness of the psyche to all sensory stimuli. As one attempts to think of a pencil, the body is too hot, uncomfortable in sitting or standing; a bell rings, someone sneezes —and off the mind goes in response. Or the chain associations noted in the recall exercise assert themselves, and it becomes almost impossible to hold the attention on the chosen subject. All this is merely habitual; it is not innate in the nature of the mind. The mind can be taught to enjoy reflecting the quietude of the inner consciousness or resting in one idea, just as it has in the past been taught to respond quickly to a variety of outward stimuli. But the re-education requires repeated effort and considerable time.

The result will be achieved the more quickly if the student practices concentration of attention on what he is doing during the day, holding the mind quietly attentive on each little job as it comes along. Such deliberate paying of attention to the job in hand extends the period of tech-

nical training in concentration to the whole day, and so
brings quicker results as well as stimulating self-awareness.

EXERCISE SUGGESTED

(1) Review exercises mentioned in the text, such as the practice of recall (Chapter III) and comments on breathing, relaxation and different postures. Make your own experiments on these points, trying different methods and comparing the effects on your own consciousness.

(2) *Concentration on Object.* Relax; breathe quietly; make the body comfortable.

Visualize the object chosen, in this case a bottle of ink of a brand you know. See its correct shape, its label, its color. Note whether it is full or empty. Have an actual bottle to study at first, if need be, and study its color, its contour, its base, its top.

Close the eyes and mentally picture the object, the nearest side first, then from the back, from above, from below. When you can see it completely in the mind, let the mind rest, identified with the object. Hold the thought form as a whole steadily in the mind, for at least a minute, more if possible—up to *three minutes.*

It will probably need practice to visualize the total object, however simple it may be. The ability to do this will grow through repeated effort, and is a useful form of thought control.

If the effort is successful, it is possible for the image to persist for some time afterward. If this proves so persistent as to be a nuisance, break up the image deliberately, and use the will to erase it each time it reappears.

POINTS FOR CONSIDERATION

(1) Why is the practice of concentration difficult?
(2) What is the relative value of conentrating on an impersonal object, or on one with an emotional content?

(3) What is the importance of concentrating full attention upon a task, and not thinking of other activities while doing it?

(4) Consider the use of the will as a deleting agent. (See pages 55-56.)

BOOKS FOR STUDY

As mentioned in the text and also:

Concentration, An Approach to Meditation	Ernest Wood
Mind and Memory Training	Ernest Wood
Concentration and Meditation, Part One	Buddhist Society
Meditation for Beginners, Section on Concentration	J. I. Wedgwood

Chapter V

PROGRESSIVE STAGES: MEDITATION, CONTEMPLATION

To mount to God is to enter into oneself. For he who so mounting and entering goes above and beyond himself, truly mounts up to God. The mind must then raise itself above itself and say, He whom above all I need is above all I know. And so, carried into the darkness of the mind, gathering itself into that all sufficient good, the mind learns to stay so at home and with whole affection cleave and become habitually fixed in the supreme good within. So do, until you become immutable and arrive at that true life which is God himself: perpetually, without any vicissitude of space or time reposing in that inward quiet and secret mansion of the Deity.
Albert, Bishop of Ulm,
Teacher of St. Thomas Aquinas

There is a clear distinction between concentration and meditation, although the two are often associated in practice. In concentration the intention is to understand and to control the mind so that it no longer reacts restlessly to incident as in the past; instead, at the behest of the Self, it is taught to sustain steady attention even upon quite dull subject matter. Concentration exercises are a technical re-education of the lower mind, so that it becomes obedient to the Self, and ceases to flit hither and thither.

In meditation the purpose is to train the mind, now quieted, to rest on a chosen subject, preferably of deep or spiritual significance, so that that subject may unfold to the meditating consciousness its richer meanings. Concentration upon mundane affairs only merges into meditation when the *truth* about the matter is sought. In other words, meditation is an invocation of subtler mental activity, the concept meditated upon being held germinating in the mind until some inner significance becomes evident.

Thus the purpose of meditation is at least two-fold. It is used to awaken the intuitional activities of the mental life, to make habitual thinking more illumined, more truthful than hitherto. At the same time it cultivates qualities that nurture and express the spiritual man. Further, the change in mental habit may lead to an intuitive approach to all problems, and the growth of insight and serenity can, in time, establish an open line of communication between the waking consciousness and its spiritual source, its Father in Heaven.

THE TECHNIQUE OF INTUITIVE RESEARCH

The technique of intuitive research, or the use of the intuition to learn the truth about puzzling material, conflicting duties and the like, requires as preliminary preparation the practice of concentration and the development of a considerable degree of impersonality. The achievement of all this has been discussed very fully in theosophical literature.* If impersonality and some degree of concentration are present when a problem presents itself to a student or aspirant, the mind can then be made to review all the aspects of the matter in hand with detachment, its effects

*See *At the Feet of the Master* under Discrimination, Control of Mind, etc.; *Spiritual Life for the Man of the World*, Annie Besant.

upon others as well as upon oneself, its roots in the past, its possibilities for the future. For a scientific, literary or technical problem, so far as is reasonably possible, *all* relevant material should be reviewed. This is necessary in order to prepare, to tune in, the lower mind. It has to supply and arrange material wherewith to state the question in full and truly. Later it may need just this same material and background to enable it to unfold and express the insight obtained.

When all the elements of the problem have been sifted and analyzed, a flash of understanding may result—usually a common sense solution arising from a purely rational process. If not, then an appointment should be made with one's higher Self, at a time suitable for quiet meditation, with the intent to reach a deeper level of comprehension. At the agreed moment, after briefly reviewing the co-ordinated material, let the consciousness rest in a large view of the whole matter, lifting the problem into the realm of silent wordless cogitation. Empty the personal mind and wait for further enlightenment. The truth exists: the right solution can be known. Wait for it to make itself clear.

If the effort is successful, there will come a flash of illumination, a glimpse of a possible new view of the facts, or—if this has been desired—the outline of a lecture. Sometimes this is clear, sometimes ill-defined. Assimilate whatever comes and repeat the experiment at a later date if need be. Often in the interval a tiny fragment of understanding, a vague glimpse, defines itself more clearly and expands into full comprehension. When sudden full insight occurs, as it may, it requires considerable time to register this clearly in the lower mind, to express it in words. Much of the material acquired beforehand may then prove useful, rearranged and readjusted to express the new insight.

The second use of meditation is the more usual. Many students desire to cultivate qualities or modes of reaction that will express the real Self in daily life. In the past these may have been expressed incidentally, but they have not been deliberately nurtured. Now it is desired to develop them more rapidly. It is true that the value of such deliberate culture has been challenged by some modern psychologists, who fear that it may produce a purely artificial state of mind, which may assert that the good and the true exist, but nevertheless leaves a personal condition of distrust or anxiety unchanged. There is a genuine problem here: the psychologists' challenge cannot be ignored. A mere mental repetition of a phrase—for example, that God is love, and that all people are his children—does nothing but mislead the one making such a verbal assertion. If some comprehension of the meaning of universal love is desired, one must—sincerely and deeply—press back into the meaning, the reality within the words, until there is an assimilation of the quality, or experience, that these words imply and a consequent change in the mental and emotional nature. Only when such assimilation begins to take place can the effort be termed meditation.

Subjects suitable for such meditations obviously differ from those chosen for concentration, although at the beginning of any meditation it is useful to concentrate for some minutes upon the objective aspect of the subject. Qualities of soul, such as kindness, courage, courtesy, perseverance, and so on, are suitable for this work, but each student will choose for himself, either what he feels himself to need, or subjects indicated by circumstances.

The usual preliminary of relaxation and easy breathing is valuable, followed by a few moments given to sustained concentration on the meaning of the chosen quality, its usual method of expression, or particular personal examples. This tunes the mind to the note required. For the beginner this will in all probability be the longest part of the exercise.

True meditation begins when the thought or concept can be allowed to lie quietly in the mind, while its essential nature is *experienced,* like a tune sung or a wind blowing over the soul. Consciousness then becomes soaked in its essence and expanded by awareness of its overtones. Often a quite new comprehension of the idea will arise, as for example when a woman who was full of fear meditated on courage, and at last came to the point where she exclaimed: "I thought courage was screwing yourself up to face horribly unpleasant situations, but it's not! It is letting yourself drop back into life!"

To be effective, meditation upon the same virtue or concept needs to be repeated daily, perhaps for a month or more. Later it may be necessary to return to the same meditation over and over again for long periods, if the quality is to grow roots in the character and take the place of an opposite weakness. Imperfections of character have probably remained unchallenged for many lives: it is not to be expected that they can be completely eliminated even in a year, much less in a fortnight. The first effect, indeed, is often to make one so aware of the weakness that it seems stronger than ever. This is illusory. The difficulty may, however, be thrown to the surface, and so become more obvious.*

As in concentration, little can be achieved unless one also expresses the desired quality in daily contacts. A morning meditation can strike a keynote, but mundane affairs will drown all trace of that note unless, throughout the day, life is lived afresh, expressing the new rhythm. This aspect of meditation invokes the spiritual will just as much as does the practice of concentration.

Meditation can be carried on as a pure science, as has been stated, without devotion to any personal ideal. But devotion does help, and those to whom the existence of spiritual teachers seems reasonable will be stimulated by turning to them, and reaching out toward the ideal that they so strongly represent, during some phase of the daily meditation. Those who feel devotion to the Christ can do much by lifting heart and mind into his presence.†

Only as one is regular in practice and persistent in application will noticeable changes in the personal nature take place. But they do occur, as thousands can testify. Regular meditation and practice on the lines indicated can enable the eye of the soul to open again upon the world of the spirit, because the daily practice gradually accustoms the soul to turn to the Self for guidance when in any difficulty. The soul then realizes that the light of the Self always shines within each one of us; the limited waking consciousness usually is not aware of it, but it is there.

*In the Outer Court, by Annie Besant. Chapters on "Building of Character" and "Spiritual Alchemy."
†In Meditation for Beginners, J. I. Wedgwood, see chapter on "The Search for the Master."

"...to know
Rather consists in opening out a way
Whence the imprisoned splendour may escape
Than in effecting entry for a light
Supposed to be without...."*

The practice of meditation can be effective in "opening out a way." It is for this purpose that it has been designed.

CONTEMPLATION

Little can be written on this stage of experience, for its objective is to carry the consciousness beyond the range of thought, and leave it not only open to, but feeling its unity with, the one Life. Conscious *samadhi,* or complete absorption in the Infinite, is said by Patanjali to take place when "the succession of the modifications of the gunas (natural processes) comes to an end"; it is "the return of the power of pure consciousness to its essential form."† It is obvious that little of any value can be written on such matters, but when the neophyte is ready, he will find the necessary guidance unexpectedly near at hand.

Paracelsus by Robert Browning.
†*Patanjali:* IV, 34; Dvivedi translation.

EXERCISE IN MEDITATION

Meditation upon a characteristic, in this case kindliness.

Relax and breathe as before; feel the body as resting easily.

Take the word *kindliness* and savor it for a time, extracting its deeper meaning, e.g. consideration for others, the effort to understand, goodwill in practice, tenderness, gentleness, etc.

If no synonyms come to mind, or for a change after some days, think of kindly people whom you know, and try to get the feeling of the way they look at life. They are gentle, do not make trouble, are interested in other people's views, do not judge harshly, etc.

Pass in thought to the kindliness taught and shown by the Great Ones; the story of the good Samaritan, the care of the Christ for his mother and friends, his gentleness to children, to the suffering. If you know similar traditions concerning other great Teachers, consider these.

Pause and feel personal kindliness for those with whom you associate. Withdraw deeply into your higher Self and feel kindliness for all, a pure impersonal kindliness radiating in all directions, without special object.

Take a few easy deep breaths, and retain the feeling of general kindliness when you get up to do other things.

This exercise can be repeated for a week or even a month, and will grow richer in meaning and in effect, if the quality is also expressed in daily life.

POINTS FOR CONSIDERATION

(1) Consider the stages of intuitive meditation:
   (a) Survey of field.
   (b) Rational arrangement of material.
   (c) Moment of listening and receptivity.

(d) Clarification of new viewpoint.

Why does the development of impersonality assist this technique? How does concentration help?

Name some factors or conditions that are likely to prevent its successful operation.

(2) Why is concentration on the chosen subject useful as a preliminary to meditation?

EXERCISE IN CONTEMPLATION

Contemplation of Divine Man.

Make the usual preparation, rather more fully, putting the physical body at ease.

If possible read something you find stimulating or illuminating in regard to the Divine Man (John xiv, 9-15; xv, 1-13; *Bhagavad Gîtâ X*, etc.) or recite a short verse if very much to the point.

Feel peace and goodwill to all.

Meditate on the existence of spiritual teachers of all races and lands, devoted to human service and to the revelation of truth.

Think of the Divine Saviors, the Avatâras or revealers of the Divine Life. They come forth to the world to bring compassion, understanding, unity. They show what human nature can become; they reveal all that the human form can show of the Divine Nature.

Contemplate the Christ, and in stillness draw near to his Presence. Open the heart to his light, his blessing.

Rest in the peace of the Presence without words, letting it alter you, nourishing the spirit within you.

"That Thou art, that may I become!"

* * *

Turn outward and let the blessing of the Master flow through you to all who suffer, to those you love, to those you find difficult; to all in authority, that they may be wise, illumined.

* * *

Let his blessing cleanse and steady your mind, your feelings, your physical body. Carry the blessing with you as you go back to ordinary work.

———————

If you should be interrupted, take a deep breath before moving, do not allow yourself to come back with any feeling of resistance or anxiety.

Do not speak to anyone of any interior experience. If you have need of expression, write it for yourself alone to read. If you have need of advice, seek someone who is wise in such matters and not merely a personal friend.

BOOKS FOR STUDY

Volumes have been written on this subject. The Buddhist Society's book *Concentration and Meditation,* already referred to, gives a maximum of material in small compass, with valuable hints based upon long experience on the part of seekers for enlightenment.

Introduction to Yoga	Annie Besant
Practical Mysticism	˙Evelyn Underhill

See also references given in the chapter.

Chapter VI

OBSTACLES AND AIDS

Happy is the man who, by continually effacing all images and who by introversion and the lifting up of his mind to God, at last forgets and leaves behind all images....See then that your whole exercise about God within you depends wholly and only on your naked intellect, affection and will. For indeed this exercise cannot be discharged by any corporeal organs or the external senses but by that which constitutes (essentially) man — understanding and love.   Albert, Bishop of Ulm
For we have somehow to discern the true way of the Lord from among the tangled lanes and the arterial highways which run in every direction or none: must learn to distinguish the enduring reality from the sham. This deep experimental knowledge of the things of God—at the opposite pole from all notional spirituality, all religious cleverness—develops and becomes more precise as we seek to apply it.   THE GOLDEN SEQUENCE, *Evelyn Underhill*

The student has by now realized that training in thought control constitutes a science, and that there are aspects of its more advanced stages which can only be understood as one's experience increases. In many studies, and especially in scientific work, elementary individual experiment is essential before advanced technique can be employed. This is certainly true of the use of meditation, because intelligent thought control makes the practitioner progressively more aware of the behavior of his interior consciousness. He soon begins to recognize some of the deep-rooted automatisms of his body, of his feelings, of his mind, and to appreciate the difficulty of directing attention along new lines. Growth, progress, movement in the new direction—call it what you will—depends from then on upon determination to carry on and upon willingness to sacrifice the familiar, the habitual, for the sake of spiritual adventure.

Thus the chief obstacle to success in meditation is the usual resistance of the personal nature to the formation of new habits. It will be useful to study this in more detail.

RESISTANCE OF THE BODIES

Each of the personal bodies has grown up on the path of outgoing, a phase of growth when it is entirely natural to place the emphasis on the outer rather than on the inner worlds. During this period each of the bodies has been fed, stimulated, sustained in its own nature, mainly through external contacts. The physical world is then, usually, the chief if not the only one to which the consciousness using the bodies "pays attention." To turn this attention away from personal and worldly matters, and to direct it toward the life of the spirit certainly requires effort.* Moreover each body has its own elemental life, and it is sometimes said that "the elementals team up" to prevent radical change taking place, because such change means the de-

*Compare Chapter II, and reference page 25, Chapter I.

struction of their habitual patterns and the building of new ones. So mind, feelings, and the physical body too, will present all sorts of excuses for *not* meditating. If the practice is continued, then they will take any chance to interfere. The body will fidget; the emotions worry over the breakfast ahead, its preparation or its time scheme; while the mind will present shopping lists, interesting reading, and the illness of relatives. The mind supports the emotions; the emotions stir the mind.

If the student knows that this is normal, he will not be discouraged. Let him look at the interruptions calmly, observe their type and source, and dismiss them again and again. If necessary agree to deal with them later. "All right: I'll attend to you after breakfast, but not *now*."

The practice of recall is helpful here.* It is also helpful to see clearly the problem involved in changing the focus of attention from the without to the within, and to realize that listening to the without leads to excitement, change, worry: whereas, when listening to the within, only quietude will enable one to hear. All that has been said previously about the use of odd moments, and of the value of concentration on whatever one is doing during the day, applies to the struggle with the bodies. It *is* a struggle: hitherto they have run loose following their own inclinations. Now they must be broken in to follow the will of the Self, and it needs time and determination to bring them under control.

As a rule too little emphasis is laid upon the process by which the psyche is to be released from, or emptied of, its old ways. It is important not to fight too laboriously against an obstacle, for it can feed on the element of self

*Exercise for Chapter III.

interest that is then involved, and so become strong in opposition through the very emphasis laid upon its continued existence. Clearance is a dual process, a turning away from the old pattern of thought or feeling and a filling of the consciousness with new life of a chosen quality. The two should run concurrently, at least at first. In time the student may learn a quick knack of rejection, which can be almost instantaneously effective. If because of type, or of previous training, the will can be used to delete *and forget* quickly, all that is needed is the vision that sees what must be deleted, and then it can be got rid of at once. But the vacuum created must be filled, automatically or deliberately, or the difficulty may recur, sometimes in quite subtle disguise.*

ENVIRONMENT

It is a great help, when attempting a subtle task of this nature, to be among others who either use, or are sympathetic to, the same methods. That was, and still is, one of the assets of the monastic life. Monks and nuns can expect to receive expert direction concerning the difficulties of the spiritual life, including those encountered in private prayer and meditation. Some religious directors give advice also to laymen who ask for it, and in the East there are many schools of yoga, as well as monasteries. For the ordinary westerner, however, busy earning a living or keeping house for others, the experiment is often attempted under difficult conditions.

Thought Power by Annie Besant, Chapters VI and VII (Quest Book edition); *Introduction to Yoga:* Lecture IV; *The Play of Consciousness* by E. L. Gardner: Chapter on "Will and Mind." See also exercises for this chapter.

Learning to pick up and drop study or other interesting work without irritation is excellent training for the bodies, but serious meditation requires solitude, and, without making his requirements conspicuous, an earnest student should be able to arrange for a short *uninterrupted* period of quiet for this purpose. The best time is the early morning before eating. Late evening is not a useful time for such work for many reasons, although a brief period of chosen reading before sleep is helpful.

The value of a moment of quiet, easy breathing and of relaxation, taken before meditation, has been noted. The question of posture is often raised. Any posture *that leaves the spine upright,* and allows for full relaxation of the rest of the body, will do, even kneeling, if the body is used to this and can relax in that position. Lying down is not good, for it tends to negativity or even to falling asleep. The eastern cross-legged position is a perfectly balanced one, if comfortable, but sitting in a suitable chair, with upright spine, may be better for westerners. The combination of the upright spine, which assists a positive mental attitude, with deep relaxation of the other parts of the body, exactly illustrates the state of poise between extremes that is most to be desired in meditation.

The general health should be studied, and the effect of thought and feeling upon bodily vigor. Since anxiety and mental strain tend to create nervous fatigue, the quieting of mind and emotions naturally brings about a release of vitality. Any exercise that appears to strain the heart, or leaves a tendency to headache, should be queried, and if the difficulty cannot be overcome by further relaxation, these particular exercises should not be used.

Nervous overstrain can occur from too great intensity in regard to the whole subject of occult study, and shows itself in digestive troubles, headaches, hypertensions, twitchings, and the like. It may be relieved by the practice of deep relaxation, learning to work with greater impersonality, with less self-interest, less desire to excel, and so on. Occasionally a particular method is not suited to a given individual, or the body is not healthy enough to take the training. On such matters expert advice should be obtained.

On no account should attention be focused upon the psychic centers of the body, for these are easily disturbed and such disturbance is dangerous to health and sanity, and also hard to cure.*

The purely negative method of "sitting for development" recommended by certain groups for the purpose of establishing some form of psychic communication with the next world, should not be used. It is best not to seek psychic powers directly. They arise naturally at a considerably later period, and are then positive; that is they are then under conscious control. The words *positive* and *negative* sometimes puzzle students. How can one be positive and yet listen to the voice of the inner Self?

In this connection the term negative is used to indicate an attitude that voluntarily renounces control of the personal bodies, loosens the actual structure of these bodies and then waits with the hope that "something will happen," i.e. that some external entity will take charge and make its ideas known by automatic writing, or other means *not* under the control of the recipient. Positive psychism, on the other hand, demands that full self-direction shall

*See reference page 44, Chapter III.

always be maintained. The recipient knows what he is doing and makes his own adjustments. Different centers are used for the two methods, and the material of the bodies is differently arranged.

In positive psychic experience, it is the finer layers of matter that react to the inner perceptions, technically the higher sub-planes of each plane, and it is the heart and the head centers that are normally employed. The training indicated in this course of study prepares the bodies ultimately for the development of positive psychic perception, for the denser matter is thrown out of the personal vehicles, and the subtle heart and head centers tend to become active. Psychic experience is unlikely to come quickly, perhaps not even in this life, but if and when it does take place it would be of the positive type. Wedgwood gives a useful discussion of this point, in *Meditation for Beginners.**

There is likely to be discouragement, from time to time, over the failure to achieve quick results, and this has to be dealt with patiently. For most people, and especially for those who feel it to be a new adventure, meditation exercises are not likely to bring about psychic visions. Many authorities point out the ease with which the desire to shine among one's fellows in the world at large can shift to a desire to be exceptional in the spiritual world. It is a fact that a serious student, who in this life once more turns to the study of the inner life, may almost immediately have some slight contact with a leader or teacher, some experience that assures him that he is on the right track. Then nothing further of that kind may occur for years. It is a waste of time to seek such experiences, or to be discour-

Meditation for Beginners, Wedgwood: Section "Positivity and Psychic Development"; see also *Varieties of Psychism* by the same author.

aged if they do not take place. And one does well to beware of self-delusion, such as interpreting bright sunlight shining upon closed eyes as an astral illumination, exaggerating the occasional feeling of exaltation into a marvelous experience, and so forth. Such happenings should be explained on physical grounds if possible: if there is genuine evidence for non-physical contacts, let them be pondered in the heart and not made unduly important.

Stunts of any kind, such as special breathing, fasting, long hours of study, exaggeration of any element in the work, are certainly to be avoided. They easily lead to nerve strain, self-delusion or worse, and are only another temptation on the part of the bodies, or of egoism, in order to get a little personal excitement out of an otherwise somewhat tedious task.

The golden mean between zeal and inertia is—as always—the ideal. Here, it involves impersonal sustained effort, like that of a good walker who knows how long he can keep up a certain pace, sets that pace, and keeps to it.

On no account should the student turn away from life. Meditation exercises are essentially an aspect of life. They are a method of training for more effective work in the world. When the bodies become disciplined and more responsive to the spiritual will, the student may develop greater insight into the needs of others, and be able to deal with his own problems more wisely. When those about him see that daily meditation makes a co-worker or a relative kinder, more understanding and friendly, more capable of giving intelligent help if that is needed, they will have a better opinion of the way of life that he has chosen.

"There is only one life—the 'spiritual' life consists in laying hold on it in a particular way so that action becomes charged with contemplation, and the Infinite is served in and through finite things."*

EXERCISES SUGGESTED

(1) Sometimes special difficulties are very persistent. Face the problem involved squarely and try to get down to its deep roots, giving it a true name. For example, shyness often is linked to egotism; resentment of injustice to others is usually related to one's own frustrations, fears, etc. Try to get beneath the surface of the trouble, however unpleasant the effort may be. Do not brood over it, but give it direct attention and deal with it creatively.

If this is not successful, then trace the feeling back into earlier life. This is an old monastic exercise, though nowadays made familiar by modern psychology. *When did I feel like this before? recently; in adolescence; in earliest childhood?* Let associated ideas and pictures float quietly in the mind. Do not hunt for them. In time, if the method is successful, some buried memory may arise, something long forgotten, almost always associated with strong emotion. Allow the emotion full sway; feel it all over again. Often there is an infantile sense of impotence or misery. Let it register fully.

When the emotion has worked itself out, look at the experience as from the present day. That was normal to the child; inevitable, perhaps, under all the then conditions. *Do I need to keep repeating that feeling now?* One can review the situation comparatively, keeping entire sympathy for the child's experience, but choosing to be different now. To get rid of the effect may need some definite cultivation of another view of parents, friends, or

The Golden Sequence by Evelyn Underhill.

situations, such as deeper understanding or greater love. It may need a special choice of meditation for a while to build the new view. Sometimes there can be an almost miraculous release from deep-seated tensions; sometimes it takes years to eradicate them. But it helps to see their origin, to date them; and then to see that the adult can choose to cultivate other ways of feeling. It is a wonderful fact that real love, without desire for recognition or return, can act as a solvent for many old bondages and tensions. Where karma permits, simple acts of goodwill and service toward those associated with the difficulty will help to establish the new relationship. But do not expect quick results.

A word of warning must be added against all forms of public or group self-analysis, whatever name may be given to them. At certain psychiatric clinics, group discussion of early conditions is sometimes encouraged, but always under guidance of a highly qualified psychiatrist. No objection is raised to such treatment. But a fashion has recently come into vogue in several countries of semi-public confession of early memories, called up by free association of ideas, with at best an unqualified practitioner present from one of these self-analytical cults. Such meetings should be avoided for many reasons. The most obvious is their crude exhibitionism; the most important is that for some natures there is genuine danger of sudden release of normal inhibitions. Hysteria and even complete loss of self-control may result, and once let down, it is not easy to restore the normal protective barriers used by consciousness to contain those unassimilated forces that exist, unrecognized, in many natures. Should deep analysis be required, it should be sought individually from qualified persons, not amateurs, and not in public.

(2) *The Doctrine of the Act.* An interesting chapter under this heading will be found in *Concentration and Meditation* (Buddhist Society, London). It is a fact that life is fulfilled by living it, and not by trying to escape from one aspect of life to another. The final answer to frustration, discontent and the like, lies wholly within oneself. Through the discovery of one's own potential wholeness, of what Berdyaev would perhaps call the uncreated freedom of the human consciousness, there arises the possibility of creative relationships with others, and within oneself.

The valuable practice, technically called "the doctrine of the act," helps one to accept life as it is for the moment, neither desiring more, nor rejecting what one has. It should be used only when the student has become familiar with the simpler forms of concentration, and has developed to some extent the power of sustained thought upon one subject. It may be summarized as follows.

While doing any small act, try to remain completely aware of the whole range of your consciousness. Accept the situation, giving it your complete attention. It is possible, with practice, to maintain awareness of the sensory responses, say in washing up dishes, of the feelings aroused, and of the activity of the mind also, so that one savors the full chord of that instant of being. This calls out the will-in-action, and can be a whole-making or healing experience. The material on the will in Chapter IV should be considered again in connection with this exercise.

It may be that using the exercise will tend to alter not only some of the reactions—which may be seen as wasteful—but even the choice of activities. In any case it should be employed for pleasant, dull, and unpleasant experiences. Repeat *ad lib*. Its value increases with repetition.

POINTS FOR CONSIDERATION

(1) Consider the resistance of the bodies to change, taking each in turn and considering what it fears and what it usually desires.

(2) Do you find the practice of recall useful in getting rid of intruding thoughts?

(3) Does the body tend to get tense in meditation? If so why? Study the way the will brings about the act of relaxation, stiffening and relaxing a muscle, say of the arm, and observing carefully the difference in the effort to increase tension and in the act of letting go.

(4) Distinguish clearly between positive and negative methods of psychic development. (See *Varieties of Psychism*, Wedgwood.)

(5) Consider the relation between meditation and daily life.

BOOKS FOR STUDY

Hints on the Study of the Bhagavad Gîtâ	Annie Besant
Gods in Exile	J. J. Van der Leeuw
Mount Everest	George Arundale
Steps in Spiritual Growth	Basil Wilberforce
The Golden Sequence	Evelyn Underhill

Chapter VII

GROUP MEDITATION

The reasonable part of the soul is not subject to the genii (elementals), it is designed for the reception of God, who enlightens it with a sunny ray.

Hermes, quoted in THE SECRET DOCTRINE I, 334

Meditation used by a group of suitable people has some advantages and some disadvantages, when compared with individual effort. In private meditation one can follow one's own timing, choosing one's own subject and line of thought. In a group that is well knit, either from temperament or from the members' adaptation to each other, the group consciousness supports the personal effort, and more effective work can be done in the way of contacting and distributing useful influences. To do this, however, individuals have to fall in with the general movement of the group and not follow personal preferences. If one has a strong personal feeling against directed meditations it is advisable not to take part in them.

Some people fear the strain of group meditation, but in our opinion there is no danger if the combined thought is guided from stage to stage, and given a positive quality both of aspiration and of dedication. Long periods of silence are *not* advisable, unless the persons taking part are habituated to such stillness, as they are in the Society of Friends. There are two reasons for this. On the one hand, without direction a group consciousness may not shape itself. Those taking part then remain merely an aggregate of individuals thinking their own separate thoughts, however beautiful and friendly these may be. To call such activity a group meditation is inaccurate. On the other hand, if a thought-entity forms during a long sustained stillness, it is possible for the devic life to become rather overwhelming, and without a directed distribution this can cause individual emotionalism, or even group hysteria. Hence the need for direction, first to bring thought together, then to steady it, and finally to distribute the group life effectively.

Meditation in a mixed public meeting, as, for instance, before a public lecture, has little or no value; indeed it often makes a new arrival feel self-conscious or restive.

In the meditation of any group meeting with spiritual intent, the thought of the members is at least somewhat attuned, and certain ideals may be assumed to be held in common. Here group meditation can have real value. Regular attendance is a great help.

The suggestions made here are all based upon considerable experience with thoughtful people of common interests, gathered at summer schools or study weekends, where lectures and discussion meetings were also held. At such places a short group meditation early each day has proved valuable.

The group being seated comfortably, the most effective sequence is (a) unification of the group; (b) offering of the unit for service; (c) aspiration and invocation of blessing; (d) distribution. Five to ten minutes is ample for the whole sequence, as few mixed groups can sustain such work effectively for a longer time.

In a small group the leader needs no more than to be familiar with the outline of the meditation that is to be used, and to read or recite it with simplicity and dedication. Several forms will be appended, all of which have been tested many times. For a newly formed group it is best to begin with that which has the most clearly marked sequence (see exercise for this chapter, pages 88-89), and to use this until it becomes easy for the members to work together.

In more detail: the preparation should begin by each member relaxing the physical body and getting it into a comfortable position; then easing the emotional nature, feeling warmth and kindliness for all present and for the world at large. This is followed by stilling the mind, and offering the whole consciousness to the work in hand. In a trained group these stages need not be noted; a general instruction, to relax tensions and attempt to make a unity, is all that is needed, with a moment's pause to allow this to be done.

With experience a leader learns to time his few words so that an average speed is maintained. Some people like a long time for each adaptation; others do it instantaneously by an act of will. Inevitably each must adapt to the whole, and the leader needs to study his members, and even to ask, at first, if they would like more or less time. *It is impossible for all to be suited:* find an average.

The act of dedication can be achieved in various ways. In a mixed gathering the idea need only be slightly touched upon, because some people become shy and self-conscious if the group work becomes too devotional or per-

85

sonal. It is usually enough to suggest the offering of the common life as a unit, for the service of the world. Where a purpose is already agreed, as in a healing group, and if dedication to this purpose has become habitual, the instant of rededication can merely be indicated as a fresh and joint offering.

The third point in the sequence, that of invoking contact with a high ideal, and the receiving of a blessing, is even more difficult to indicate clearly when there is a mixed membership. Nor in these days can one always rely upon the acceptance of a purely Christian outlook or terminology. In large mixed groups some general term may be employed, such as "one's highest ideal." On the other hand in smaller groups where the beliefs of members are known, more specific reference to the Christ, or to other spiritual teachers may be entirely suitable.

If the unification is effective and the dedication sincere, there tends to arise at this point, or even earlier, a sustained sense of unity, of release and of quietude, which indicates the linking of the subtle bodies of those present into a temporary group entity. An entity of this type is always formed and enhanced by angelic influences. Such influences have various qualities, and at times great power.

While at many such meetings the existence of an "over-soul" is an undoubted fact, it should not be sought consciously, nor talked about afterward, or its value is dissipated. Even in a small lodge, the life contacted by sincere group meditations can be surprisingly strong, for it depends upon dedication, and not upon large numbers, skill or learning. The angels wait for opportunities to co-operate with mankind; we give them too few. Even mighty devas are attracted to, and enhance, a group manifestation that is harmonious and of idealistic quality, and this is especially so where their presence is taken for granted. There are, however, other types of influence. There are lesser entities who enjoy personal excitement and over-emotionalism, or are attracted by psychic curiosity and foolish talk about the inner worlds. Such influences can lead to hysteria, and to the inflation of personal importance. So if a blessing be felt, or the presence of unseen influences noted, let it be taken for granted. Helpful unseen members of the group will come and do their work, and then depart with mutual blessing and goodwill, just as do the visible members. Whether they are perceived, or work unrecognized, does not matter. It is a law of the inner life that no pure channel is ever opened for its use that is not at once filled and used to the utmost. There is need for such channels; there is a pressure, as it were, in the world of the spirit, and no outlet could be overlooked, any more than water could fail to flow through an opening in a full reservoir. It may happen at times that some element is present in a group—ill health, ill feeling, or some undercurrent—that checks contact with the inner worlds, just as there are meetings when such contacts are unusually strong. Again it is better not to discuss this in the group, but merely to do whatever can be done to provide the best conditions for the work. As with personal meditation, the use of group meditation is a science. It may be approached in a devotional spirit, certainly, but its technique can also be studied quite impersonally. Experiment with various forms provides a means of studying the effect of different arrangements, formulae and methods.

On the whole it is not advisable to mix different kinds of work in one group meeting. For example, use of some form of group meditation to help the world at large, should not include at the same meeting special healing thought for a member who may be ill. Individual members may include a friend in their consciousness, as sharing in the group activity; or members may include in their personal thought during the distributive period the will to be of use to those near them in daily life. But the healing of individual people is a special task that needs some training, and on the whole it is better not to include it in a general group meditation held for other purposes. (See next Chapter)

Some may care to join in those moments of dedication, such as dawn, noon and sunset, used throughout the world by all religions. In periods of crisis, such common thought becomes noticeably stronger.

To sum up: it is clear that groups may be effective centers for the concentration and distribution of spiritual power. The technique, like any other useful activity, needs both study and practice. In these days of confused thinking, distress and uncertainty, dedicated group thought can certainly be of use in releasing streams of cleansing and stabilizing spiritual life. Harmonious meetings for this purpose strengthen the organization that does the work as well as the members who share in the effort.

———————

EXERCISE SUGGESTED

(1) Let members sit comfortably in their seats; relax the eyes, the back of the neck, the spine and limbs. Take two or three quiet easy breaths. *Leader says quietly:* "My body is resting...but I am not my body." *Pause.*

"The emotions are strong, urgent. I choose to feel at peace, quiet, resting." *Pause.* "I am not my emotions; I can control and direct them. I send out goodwill and warmth to the whole group, and to all around me." *Pause.*

"The mind is active and full of pictures. I can direct its activity. Let it think of a wide view, a sunlit sea or valley. Let it be still, peacefully contemplating a great space." *Pauses as needed.*

(2) "Let us dedicate ourselves to the work in hand. The Self in each is pure, strong, one with all other Selves." *Pause.*

(3) "Let us lift the life of the group as a whole into the presence of the highest idea we know (or of the Lord Christ), and offer it for service. May (his) blessing rest upon us." *Pause.*

(4) "Let the light and the peace that we have received pour out to the world: *(pauses as convenient)* to all in authority that they may be wise; to all who suffer in mind, body or estate; to all we love.

"Let the peace and strength of the Self abide in our minds *(pause)* in our feelings *(pause);* and strengthen our bodies."

Members should then take a few quiet easy breaths and resume freedom of movement.

POINTS FOR CONSIDERATION

(1) Consider the advantages and disadvantages of any type of intimate collective work, such as meditation.

(2) Name the four stages of group meditation indicated in the chapter, and consider them, at first singly, and then in relation to each other.

(3) Why is it somewhat difficult to be quite natural and simple in co-operating with unseen devic workers? (See reading suggested.)

(4) Consider the work of a group as a center for blessing and for cleansing influences in the world.

BOOKS FOR STUDY

Science of the Sacraments   C. W. Leadbeater
(See index under angels, etc.)
Hidden Side of Things   C. W. Leadbeater
(See index, angels, devas, thought, etc.)
Brotherhood of Angels and of Men   Geoffrey Hodson
Nature Spirits   D. N. Dunlop
First Principles of Theosophy   C. Jinarajadasa

Chapter VIII

HELPING OTHERS BY THOUGHT

Administer ye My Life one to another. Open the gates. Shut not one of them. Acknowledge My Touch when it falls upon you. With the eyes of the soul perceive Me and be whole.

Pilgrim of the day! go forth to meet in every face the Risen One. If he wake, he will greet thee, and thy portion shall be doubled. If he slumber, hail him in silence. Wake him not. He knoweth his own hour, and God is over all.

WORDS OUT OF THE SILENCE

If one has made the effort to train the bodies so that thought can, to some extent, be controlled and directed, it is only natural that one should want to use the power of thought for helping others. But it is a delicate matter to interfere in the life of another, for all that has been said in this course indicates that the relationship between man's consciousness and the bodies it uses is not at all a simple one. Who really understands himself? How much more difficult to fathom the spiritual needs of another! One can offer what one has to give with humility and in the hope that it may be useful, but ultimately it is the recipient who decides what use is made of the assistance.

Can one human being heal another? And if so, how?

The only way that real healing can be communicated is through that which all share—that is through the life of the

Spirit.* It is the underlying life in which all are rooted that makes ordinary communication possible; permits understanding to grow between men and women of different types and differing racial backgrounds; permits a sharing of consciousness to take place so that lonely people can be cheered by others, ideas and impulses passed from mind to mind. This same basic unity allows a flow of healing power to take place from one person to another. One never—finally—heals or helps by personal activity. It is life that heals; the healer or doctor merely opens channels for life to do its work.

Release from tension, distress or pain, leading to healing, takes place in many ways. It may be instinctual and incidental, like the soothing of a terrified child by a kindly nursemaid; or it may be illumined and miraculous, like the healing work of the Christ. It may be superficial and temporary; or intentional, long sustained, and the result of professional training for such work.

So-called miracles are due to the action of law at little known levels. They can be evoked, but sometimes happen through an apparently fortuitous grouping of the necessary factors. For sustained healing work, mental or otherwise, it is good to know as much as possible of the inner laws involved. If one understands the general principles at work, one is likely to remain humble and be more impersonal. Those interested would do well to study, not merely to read, some of the recommended literature that exists on that subject.† They should attempt to distinguish the factors

*At the Feet of the Master, end of Chapter I. Some Unrecognized Factors in Medicine, Theosophical Research Centre, Chapter III and IV.

†Psychology, Religion and Healing by L. Weatherhead; New Light on Some Problems of Disease by G. Hodson; This World and That by P. and L. Bendit: Chapter X; Healing Methods Old and New by A. Gardner.

always present, and those that differ, in the following practices: vital magnetic healing; suggestion and auto-suggestion; incidental healing, such as comes from a good cry on a sympathetic shoulder; and in the complicated phenomena involved in public group healing work, such as that at places of pilgrimage or the séances of spiritualistic healers. It is always life that heals: but mechanisms vary widely, and can be at least partially understood.

The root cause of disease is a constriction of the flow of life, either from bad food, fatigue, confusion and distress of feeling, or mental tangles. Curative effort can be directed from any of these levels, structural, vital or psychological. Here we are concerned with mental or spiritual healing only. This may be attempted either in absence or with the patient near at hand. To become thoroughly efficient as a mental healer, natural fitness for the work and training are both needed, but all can do a little of it now and then, experimentally as it were, and with practice comes greater faith and increased ability to help.

Fortunately the best training for such work is precisely that needed for the growth of the spiritual consciousness and its expression in daily life, and as such it has been outlined in this study. The healer needs to relax and cleanse all his personal bodies, so that they provide an open channel for the flow of the healing life. Besides this he may offer himself to be trained for such work. A great deal of healing work is certainly done at night when out of the body, but it is done by those who have fitted themselves for it while in waking consciousness, and not at all effectively unless the training has been good.*

A basic principle in mental healing is involved in the
Invisible Helpers by C. W. Leadbeater.

inducing of a change of consciousness on the part of the patient through *(a)* a strong realization on the part of the healer of the power of life to heal; and *(b)* the projection of this released life around the patient, until he too responds to it, and consciously or unconsciously lets down the barriers that exist within himself. This corresponds very closely to the phenomenon termed induction in physics. Two coils of wire can be set up, without contact with each other. If an alternating current is sent through one coil, and the other is properly arranged in relation to the first, a current can be induced in the second, and used for further work according to its strength. The better this example is understood, the clearer will the principle become. The coils have to be suitably arranged in relation to each other; the current has to be of a certain strength to have any effect; the result will depend upon the adjustment of the second coil quite as much as upon the first. But the fact remains that energy can be transmitted from one apparatus to another, without the two being in direct dense physical contact. An example will clarify the working of the principle in healing.

A friend or patient is suffering acute depression. The healer puts himself in the right attitude of mind and body for his work. He tunes himself in to the peace and assurance of the Self. He envisages the patient as peaceful, and then as filled with the light of the higher consciousness. From the unlimited reservoir of the Life that both share, and on which they both can draw, he bathes the patient in vitality, poise, or strength, to meet his need.

If the treatment is successful, the patient feels a sense of peace welling up within him; his load of grief or self pity is for the moment lessened by the renewal of contact with the one Source of all. He is—at least temporarily—better. A new flow of energy has been *induced* from within outward, and if he picks this up and draws on it from within himself, he will continue to improve in mind, and ultimately this will help the body, if that also is suffering. If he is not properly attuned to react to the healer's effort, nothing happens. If he does not use it for himself, the effect soon fades.

Similar sharing of consciousness is going on all the time in nature and among human beings. Moods are catching, ideas float about. Some people are hard to live with, others easy, quite as much because of the mood that their presence induces in others as on account of anything overtly said or done. The healer has to become a specialist in inducing moods that heal, attitudes that release tension and so restore the flow of life right down to the level of physical prâna and the digestive fluids.

The problem of correct diagnosis is a complicated one. Many spiritual and mental healers do not try to specialize the healing thought that they send out; they leave diagnosis alone, and with great faith send love, light, life, letting the patient take what he can. There is no doubt that such an attitude, if dedicated and sincere, attracts helpers in the unseen worlds, devic or human, and that the concentrated thought evokes essential healing grace that is effectively applied by such workers, usually highly skilled at this task. This is all part of the mutual evocative life between man and the angel kingdoms, as well as among human beings alone. The powers latent in man are real, and the power to direct thought influences, so that they help and heal, is one of them.

Yet it is worth while to study the occult causes of disease

carefully, especially the science of correspondences.* An understanding of the relation between anxiety and heart trouble, between egoism and spinal pain, and so on, or of the fact that opposite psychological attitudes can produce the same result, all this is illuminating and helpful in treating special cases. With such additional knowledge the healer becomes able to specialize his thought in certain instances, and so may shorten the period of treatment, if his analysis is correct. When in doubt the general formula is the best one to use. *Such diagnosis, including as it inevitably does an element of psychological analysis, should not be offered or given to a patient unless he asks for it.*

It is, of course, illuminating also to study within oneself the relation of the true cause of disease to its cure. To become a genuine healer one does indeed need a strong, personal realization of the power of the spiritual life to effect radical changes in psychological and material conditions. Add to this, true humility in regard to oneself and a real love for others, and understanding will grow, and with that again comes an increase in the power to help and to heal.

It is a good rule to attempt such healing work at the end of one's personal meditation, since the bodies are then dedicated, unified and thus open to the flow of inner Life. Hold them steady and let them be filled with that Life, and with peace. Then name those who need help, singly, dwelling a moment upon each, and feel him or her to be bathed in healing light and strength. In special cases offer some useful quality according to the need.

Although at first it may take some time to visualize each

*Some Unrecognized Factors in Medicine: Chapter V.

person and realize life flowing out to him, one soon becomes used to the technique and can work quickly. Nor is it necessary to repeat the whole list every day. Naming a patient once a week in this way is sufficient, provided that during the interval, whenever the person comes to mind, he is held mentally in healing light.

It may seem too simple a technique to be effective, but it has been well tested. Its efficiency depends on the general principles stated above, and on certain characteristics of patient and healer. The healer needs faith, or conviction; and complete sincerity and impersonality. There is need also for patience, since in some instances the practice has to be repeated over a long period before the patient appears to benefit. The less personal feeling that is present, the better the work. The flow of life is merely distorted by longing to be of use, or fear of doing the wrong thing. As for the patient—with the best will in the world and longing to be healed—he may so confuse his relationship to the healer, or to life itself, that little effect is registered. That is the patient's business: the healer can do something to help at times, sometimes very little. Some cases have to be dropped, though fewer than might be imagined.

Mental cases are peculiarly resistant, being often a retreat from circumstances that are so unbearable that they cannot be faced. In thinking of those with mental difficulties, it is useful to try to touch one's own spiritual center, and at that level to make a bridge over to the ego, or spiritual center, of the patient, calling on him to come down and deal with his shut in, or disordered, personality; urging him to get on with his job. The ego can withdraw from a wholly unsatisfactory personality, going to sleep in devachan* as it were. Such an appeal may wake him up, but one must continue to collaborate, and to supply the personality with assistance.

Miracles of healing occur when something happens that opens the heart of the patient to wider life, or that infuses a special power into the healer. Crises, or a vital urgency, can make healers out of quite ordinary persons, as well as lift a chronic invalid into health and activity.

To work such miracles habitually is possible only for those who have utter confidence in the power that flows through them, no matter what it is called. It is this confidence that makes many spiritualists such potent magnetic healers. They feel that their "guides" are in charge and merely leave their own bodies open to be used, though the best of them work very intuitively. For conscious work one needs an equal dedication, an equal trust, repeated conscious opening of the whole being to the healing Life; but these are linked to disciplined thought and discrimination in the use of the healing power.[†]

It is best not to seek too much evidence as to results. Let the healer study his failures. There is much to be learned from them, though they are by no means always his fault.[‡]

---

*Devachan is a state of absorption in whatever one has experienced of goodness, truth, beauty, without reference to further material expression of that experience. See *Death and After*, Annie Besant: Section on Devachan.

[†]Colonel Olcott, the first President of the Theosophical Society, was a powerful healer of this type for several years. See *Old Diary Leaves* by H. S. Olcott: Vol. II.

[‡]Concerning karma and healing, see "Note on Karma and Health" at the end of *Healing Methods: Old and New*.

Group work for healing purposes is very similar to any other group meditation. To get the best results, the group should be used for this purpose only, and members should use individual meditation each day, in order to prepare their minds and feelings for the common effort. It is excellent to have an equal number of men and women, but this is not essential. Group work should not be attempted by those who themselves are ill. If a person wants to be healed, he may put his name on a healing list, or attend healing services, but he should not sit as one of those who hold meditations for the healing of others. This need not be a fixed rule, for diseases differ, but it is a sound general principle.

In all forms of group or semi-public healing work, the names and diseases of those who apply for help should be mentioned as little as possible, and all matters concerning the work should be held strictly in confidence. There are, of course, public healing services in various churches and orders. Where the laying on of hands is used, the healing becomes in part vital magnetic, as well as mental or spiritual, and the operator is then the individual priest or healer, although he may be assisted by regular attendants who come to the meetings to help through prayer or meditation, as well as by unseen agencies.

In essence the practice of healing by group thought is the same as that of group work for helping the world. Those taking part form a vessel or reservoir through the joint action of their physical (vital), emotional and mental bodies. These, being purified by aspiration and dedication to service, are linked through the common activity; and this calls out from within a special, momentary outpouring of healing influences, involving the co-operation of some rank of the healing angels, an order of devas of great significance and power. In thought, through the mentioning of initials, or the silent naming by the leader of those who have asked for help, the patient is linked to the reservoir, bathed in its life and light. Sometimes a special healing angel attaches himself to a patient and attends him for a while. The inner work is done without conscious volition on the part of the human members of the group. The human members separate and go their ways, but the inner group goes on radiating healing power, according to the development of the work and its participants. The results depend, as always, on the dedication and intelligence of the members and on the receptivity of the patient.

No one should have his name entered upon such lists without his consent. Individuals may offer help to friends without asking permission, if it be humbly and unobtrusively given, but it has been found better to confine group work to those who are willing to co-operate. Results should not be sought, nor too greatly desired. If a patient writes to say he is better, well and good; but if he is physically worse, valuable work may still have to be done. Help given may be effective in assisting the assimilation of a lesson, or in adjusting relationships with others.

It is a great privilege to work in a well-conducted group of this sort, and members learn much from the practice, both personally and in regard to healing in general.

A HEALING EXERCISE FOR PERSONAL USE

Needs at least ten minutes but should not be extended beyond half-an-hour. The first can be used to induce sleep.

Relax the physical body slowly, and as completely as possible, particularly the eyes, interior of head and back of the neck. Sit or lie heavily on the chair or floor and consciously let it support your full weight. Breathe with fully extended lungs, once or twice. Consciously relax the vital, nervous tensions (etheric body): release it on the outgoing breath and let it float out like long grass in water.

Make a deliberate effort of withdrawal from the physical and vital bodies, leaving them relaxed, at ease. Do not get exalted, but feel yourself resting in the emotional focus of consciousness. Feel your habitual tenseness there, your avidity, withdrawal, or whatever exists there. Relax this deliberately as you have done the nervous tensions. Think of sunlight, of warmth, of ease of contact with someone with whom this is established. Feel the emotional nature to be calm, opened, sustained by life.

Make a definite withdrawal from the emotional focus, and become aware of yourself as thinking. Again, relax the mind, its interior activity and quick flash from one thing to another. Let it rest in some wide view of nature. Steady the mind and let it lie still, like water in an unruffled pool, open to sunlight.

Withdraw further to the still center of the true Self. I AM...calm, serene, at ease...one with all others. Feel the unity of the Self behind all appearances. Offer your life to the service of all...to the service of your highest Ideal or Teacher. Draw near to the life of that Ideal, allow it to fill your being.

101

Pour out the peace you have found to all around you.

Return in thought to your mind, keeping it quiet and enlarged. Return to your feeling nature, feeling it to be sweetened and strong. Return to the physical frame. Take two or three deep breaths, and let energy wash through the body as you breathe in and out. Stretch shoulders and adjust the body to activity before getting up.

When the form has become familiar, variations can be made, within the general framework of the stages indicated.

POINTS FOR CONSIDERATION

(1) Consider the phenomenon described as induction and its relation to mental and spiritual healing.
(2) Consider the difference between magnetic healing and mental healing. Is it possible to distinguish clearly between these and spiritual healing?
(3) How do we influence our neighbors unconsciously?
(4) Why is it useful to study our failures, in healing work and in general?

BOOKS FOR STUDY

See list for Chapter VII, and those mentioned in references.

Chapter IX

MEDITATIONS

During the preparation of this book a good deal of useful material was collected and considered that has not been included in the text. Much of this has now been grouped in this chapter because it has value for students, or may be suitable for group use in lodges, at Study Weekends, and so on.

The additional concentration exercises explain themselves.

The outlines for group meditation have all been used, some of them many times in various groups and places, by the writer or by the person whose name has been indicated. In employing such a well-defined form, developed by another student, the leader or reader needs to get well into the feeling of the material as arranged, before attempting to use it in group. The significance of the sequence as a whole needs to be pondered, the words themselves cogitated, so that the group leader makes them his own.

The reading should be very impersonal, quiet in voice, easy, without undue emphasis, and with ample pauses. This leaves the listeners free to make their own interpretations, and gives them the time needed to do so.

In a new group, or when strangers are present, a short reading may precede the meditation outlined. A list of typical readings is added at the end. In a well-knit group, the usual instruction to relax and sit at ease is all that is needed for preparation, followed by a few minutes of silence.

(1) Select a person you are fond of and try to visualize him accurately. How much of the face can you see, how much of a characteristic gesture or carriage of the head? Keep your mind engaged in looking at one person mentally for three to five minutes if possible. If convenient, look at the actual person in between exercises in order to refresh the visual memory.

Add to the image the sense of the personal presence; what is the characteristic, to your perception, that he brings with him on entering a room? What does his handshake convey? Take one person at a time, and the same one over and over again for a week. Then change, if more interesting to have another subject.

(2) Concentrate upon some fragrance that you can actually provide in the first instance as a physical experience, say lavender water, or incense. Keep the mind attending to the smell and analyze its effect upon you in the simplest possible words. Smell the fragrance again and again and keep the attention upon the sense impressions called up. Vary the fragrance if preferred, but keep up the same exercise for a week.

(3) Use the same concentration for the sense of touch. Take material with a characteristic surface, like linen or velvet, and allow the whole consciousness to become focused in the fingertips as you run them back and forth across it. Try to keep away from the elaborate associative ideas that will tend to assert themselves, and concentrate on the bodily reaction of the senses.

These exercises are intended to establish control over attention, and to bring the will into play as director of attention and mental concentration. The result in the way of this or that intensity of experience, interesting or unpleasant, is of little importance, though it may be informative or even amusing.

Ernest Wood in *Concentration, an Approach to Meditation* gives a good exercise for the voluntary control of hearing, but this is advanced for a beginner. Taste can be studied in the same way, but it is difficult to arrange.

AN ACT OF DEDICATION
FOR PERSONAL OR GROUP USE

After preliminary relaxation:

Let us dedicate all our actions to the Master's service. *Pause.* Think of those things that bore us, that irritate us, and dedicate them as an act of service. *Pause.* Think of those tasks in which we rejoice and lose ourselves, and dedicate them, that we may learn to remember the Master in joy as well as in sorrow. *Pause.* Let us determine to remember this dedication throughout the day, in our habitual speech, gesture, and behavior. *Longer Pause.*

Let the emotions be filled with utter devotion to the Master (or to the Christ). *Usual pauses after each sentence.* Let them be "aired out" so that all feeling is clean and fresh as it is offered to him.... Let go all resentment, however slight; all sense of pressure and strain.... Let the feelings open out to him fragrantly, easily, like a wild flower. *Longer pause.*

Now steady the emotions by the dedicated mind.... Open this quietly, deliberately (toward the Master's mind.) ...Thought must be harmless, sincere, kind wherever possible, based on broad principles...and flexible. *Longer pause.*

Be still, as in the presence of the Master. Let his life make its way through you;...offer him everything....

This meditation makes a very good preparation for sending out healing thought to others.

DEDICATION OF THE SENSES
FOR PERSONAL OR GROUP USE

After preliminary relaxation say quietly with suitable pauses:

The Self in me is active in my body: it rules the senses.
I dedicate my senses to the Self, as a living sacrifice.

Smell: the physical world.

Think of early morning and the smell of flowers; the smell of food; of delicate perfume.
Breathing in, breathing out, I sense the odors of the world, noting pleasant and unpleasant.
I offer this sense to the Self.

Taste: emotions

The sense of taste tells the wholesome from the poisonous.
Hot, cold, bitter, sweet, acid, spicy; taste discerns them all.
I offer the sense of taste to the Self.

Sight: the mental world

The eye opens and shuts, the focus expands and contracts.
The eye sees and registers.
May the Self direct my sight; may the Self rule my mind!

Touch: buddhi

The sense of touch is everywhere in the body, the hands, the skin.
Rough and smooth, curved and flat, hard and soft, touch knows them all.
I offer my sense of touch to the Self. May I touch all and be one with all!

Hearing: the will

The ear listens to all sound; through it we discern the meaning of sound.

High and low, sweet and shrill, harsh and melodious— the Self in me hears all.

When I listen to the sounds of the world, may I hear the Voice of the Self!

I offer all my senses to the Self.

No distribution, but pause for some time.

GROUP MEDITATION

After usual preliminaries, say, pausing between phrases:

I am the fragrance of the earth.

The Self is One.

I am the sweetness of the waters.

The Self is One.

I am the fire of the mind.

The Self is One.

I am the joy of all touch.

The Self is One.

I am the harmony of all sound.

The Self is One.

I am all love, wisdom and will.

The Self is One.

As in the Master these glories shine out in eternal beauty to bless the worlds;

So may they shine out in us to serve and to comfort.

Josephine Ransom

GROUP MEDITATION ON LOVE

Realization

Let us realize love in its physical expression as beauty.

Pause.

Let us realize love emotionally as warmth.   *Pause.*

Love is expressed mentally as sympathy.   *Pause.*

The buddhic quality of love is understanding.   *Pause.*

Love is the Self, Atmâ; is Oneness.   *Pause.*

Love is Spiritual Radiance.

Distribution

Through the Self I express love as awareness.   *Pause.*

Through the buddhi I express love as friendliness. *Pause.*

Through the mind love shines as insight.   *Pause.*

Through the emotions love radiates as tenderness.

Pause.

Through the body love is expressed in beauty.   *Pause.*

Josephine Ransom

MEDITATION ON THE ONE LIFE AS LIGHT

BASED ON HERMETIC SENTENCES

(a) Look for the Light

"The Light is hidden everywhere; it is in every rock and in every stone. The Light is nearer than aught else, within a man's very heart. All comes forth from the Light, and to the Light all shall return."*

Look for the Light

(Pause)

(b) Follow the Light

"Follow the Light, you will reflect its radiance."†

"The sun's rays shine on all alike; he who would feel their warmth upon his skin must leave his shut-in cave and seek the open air. He who would experience the Divine Compassion in his soul must leave the cave of self and seek the wider being. He must strive upwards, outwards, from his self, breaking the barriers till the homeward-flowing tides are felt and sweep him off his feet."‡

Follow the Light

(Pause)

(c) I am the Light

"In the midst of our being stands the Lord of past and future. The inner Self is always seated in the heart of man. Let a man draw that Self forth from his body with steadiness. Let him know that Self as the Bright, as the Immortal, yea, as the Bright, as the Immortal."§

I am the Light

(Pause)

*Man, Whence, How and Whither, p. 284 et. seq. Besant and Leadbeater.

†*Tao Teh King,* Myers translation.

‡*The Yoga of the Bhagavad Gîtâ,* p. 93, Shri Krishna Prem.

§The *Upanishads.*

(d) Let the Light Shine

"Ye shall go out with joy and be led forth with peace. Arise, shine, for thy light is come and the glory of the Lord is risen upon thee."*

"The splendor of the whole world will be thine and all darkness shall flee from thee."†

Let the Light Shine

(Pause)

Dispersal

Corona Trew

MEDITATION ON THE INNER LIFE

BASED ON READINGS FROM THE *TAO TEH KING,* Myers translation

"To possess Inner Life we enter it by our own private doorway. We do this in order to know in overflowing fullness the possession of activity of Inner Life."

Inner Life is found within—let us open the doorway to that Life and enter in.

(Pause)

"If you have an ever increasing abundance of Teh (Wisdom)

Then your Inner Life is unconquerable.

If your Inner Life is unconquerable

Then its limits cannot be known.

The possessor of Tao (the Path) the Way,

Shall have enduring life and infinite vision."

Inner Life is unconquerable, illimitable, enduring and infinite.

(Pause)

"The heart of the Self-controlled man is always in the Inner Kingdom,

*Isaiah 55, 12; 60, 1.
†The Emerald Tablet of Hermes.

He draws the hearts of all men into his heart."
Abiding in the Inner Life we are at one with all.
(Pause)
Finally, turning outward to our daily world:
"Be active with the activity of Inner Life;
Serve with the service of Inner Life;
Be fragrant with fragrance of Inner Life;
His restfulness is easily maintained."
(Pause)

Dispersal

Corona Trew

MEDITATION ON PEACE
FOR USE IN GROUPS

(a) Let the bodies be relaxed and quiet *(as in exercise for Chapter VII)*.

(b) Let us remain quiet and harmonized as we offer this group as a channel for the forces of peace and goodwill to flow out to all the world....

(c) Let us feel ourselves to be in the Presence of the Lord of Life and of Love....
May his blessing rest on us....
May his peace shine through us to all mankind....
May his peace and his blessing pour out through us
to all in authority that they may be wise
and illumined.
May his love flow out to all the kingdoms of
nature...to all who suffer wrong...to all in
pain....

(d) May our minds be irradiated with his wisdom....
May our hearts be filled with his love...
our bodies with strength and serenity....

Breathe quietly and resume free movement as before.

A SHORT LIST OF READINGS

SUITABLE FOR INTRODUCING GROUP MEDITATION

Edward Carpenter, *Towards Democracy,* various extracts especially "The Lake of Beauty," Detachment," etc.

Rabindranath Tagore, *Gitanjali.*

Bhagavad Gîtâ

    II, 47-53; 70-72; IV, 7-11; 16-23. VI, 20-23; 24-28; 29-32. IX, 26-28. XII, 13-19; 26-31. XVIII, 45-49; 54-58.

Lao Tzu, *Tao Teh King.* The translation by Isabella Mears is useful for this purpose, though other translations are sometimes more forceful. The selections indicated, alone or in combination, make good introductions for group meditation, or—taken very slowly—each may form the basis of one such exercise.

    I; II; III; X; XI; XXIX, v. i, with XXXVII, v.i and XXXIV; XLV; XLVI, last verse with XLVII; XLIX; LVI with LVII, v. i; LX, v. i with LXI, v. i, iii, v; LXIII; LXXIX.

Alcyone, *At the Feet of the Master,* many suitable passages.

    Also other books recommended in Chapter I reading list for general study. The passages chosen should always be short, with a strong life quality.

Conclusion

Meditation is a life study, and the outline given here is only an introduction to the practice. No one routine could possibly suit every temperament. Each must find his own yoga, his way of integration, his path to union with the One. Mere repetition of a daily exercise is only useful at the beginning, to establish a quiet habit of mind. After the Self has become a little accustomed to taking charge of the bodies, the routine needs to be varied, experiments should be made. Only the purpose must remain inflexible: to establish a deeper insight into the nature of the Self and to confirm its directing influence upon the whole incarnate experience of the life.

Meditation may be of great practical value, since it can train the personality to be more understanding, kind, and useful in everyday affairs. It can also, as has been shown, train the mind so that it may be used directly to help others.

In the case of some students, when the mind becomes clarified, the emotions stilled, the body relaxed at will, the spirit may then attempt the exploration of vast new fields of knowledge and experience. For this, expert guidance, or at least the companionship of equals, is needed. Such help will come when the aspirant is ready for his work. Advanced forms of meditation, however, are for the few in these days. For the majority, the earlier stages are there to bring release from bewilderment and insecurity. The veil that shuts the personal nature from the Self gradually thins, the student realizes a new significance in old things,

115

new relationships with others bring tranquility where there was confusion, strength where there was weakness and doubt.

Surprisingly, one finds that the promised land is no longer far away over Jordan, but here and now, at hand. Francis Thompson expressed this in a poem found among his papers after his death.

> O world invisible, we view thee,
> O world intangible, we touch thee....
> Not where the wheeling systems darken,
> And our benumbed conceiving soars!
> The drift of pinions, would we harken,
> Beats at our own clay-shuttered doors.

Quest Books are published to help people in their search for life's meaning. Here are a few additional titles on meditation and yoga:

Approaches to Meditation
Ed. by Virginia Hanson
An anthology by meditators of different temperaments with various backgrounds.

Art of Inner Listening
By Jessie Crum
A first person account of a way to higher awareness.

Concentration
By Ernest Wood
An approach to meditation using 36 physical and mental exercises.

Creative Meditation and Multi-Dimensional Consciousness
By Lama Anagarika Govinda
On proper breathing, mantras, the esoteric structure and meaning of mandalas.

Initiation Into Yoga
By Sri Krishna Prem
An introduction to the spiritual life by a famous teacher.

Hatha Yoga
By Wallace Slater
A short guide for busy people. With diagrams.

QUEST BOOKS
306 W. Geneva Road
Wheaton, Ill. 60187